# Secret Wealth

## A Financial Plan to Share With Your Grandchildren

### Rich Hamilton

*SellBetter Tools Publishing*

*Phoenix, Arizona*

# Secret Wealth: A Financial Plan to Share With Your Grandchildren

http://SecretWealth.com

Copyright © 2015 Rich Hamilton

Published by SellBetter Tools, PO Box 50186, Phoenix, Arizona USA

ISBN-10: 0972847634    ISBN-13: 9780972847636

This publication is designed to provide accurate and authoritative information in regard to the subject matter covered. It is sold with the understanding that neither the publisher nor the author are engaged in rendering legal, accounting, or other professional services. If you require legal advice or other expert assistance, you should seek the services of a competent professional.

**All investing is subject to risk, including the possible loss of the money you invest.** The performance data featured in this book represents past performance which is no guarantee of future results. Investment return and principal value of an investment will fluctuate; therefore, you may have a gain or loss when you sell your shares. Current performance may be higher or lower than the performance data quoted.

*The mutual funds described here are for illustrative purposes only and not listed as a recommendation. You must do your own research to determine which mutual funds to buy. The performance of an index is not an exact representation of any particular investment, as you cannot invest directly in an index.*

While every precaution has been taken in the preparation of this book, the publisher and author assume no responsibility for errors or omissions. Neither is any liability assumed for damages resulting, or alleged to result, directly or indirectly from the use of the information contained herein. If you do not wish to be bound by the above, you may return this book with receipt to the publisher for a full refund of the purchase price.

Trademarks: *Secret Wealth* is not authorized by, endorsed by, or affiliated with Fidelity Investments, The Vanguard Group, their subsidiaries, or any other investment company. Fidelity is a trademark of Fidelity Investments. Vanguard is a trademark of The Vanguard Group. Other trademarks are property of their respective owners. All references to these and other trademarked properties are used in accordance with the Fair Use Doctrine and are not meant to imply that this book is a Fidelity or Vanguard product for advertising or other commercial purposes.

Schools and Corporations: This book is available at quantity discounts with bulk purchases for educational or business use. For information please contact the publisher at the address above.

## A Note for Grandparents:

In your hands you hold a simplified plan for financial success. It's not the only plan out there, but *it is the easiest plan,* combining a focused mindset with careful, systematic investing to enable your grandchildren to become *Wealth Builders* rather than *Debt Builders.*

Revealed inside:

- **How** part of everything you earn is yours to keep
- **Who** can build wealth and retire a multimillionaire
- **What** amount of money you will need at retirement
- **Why** you should keep your wealth building a secret
- **Why** the best road to wealth is *owning a business,* but owning a small business is often like buying a job
- **Why** the best business to own is a *big, successful business* like Walmart, General Electric, Coca-Cola, Disney, or Comcast
- **Why** it's *better to own a business* than to work for it
- **Why** it's safer to *own more than one business*, even hundreds of businesses
- **Where** to get the money to invest
- **When** is the best time to get started
- **How** to start a *step-by-step investment plan* expressed in understandable language

I put this plan in a letter so my granddaughters and grandson could read it, then keep to re-read as needed. My son suggested I publish it because it could help so many.

I wish I'd had this book when I started out. As you read this and see the value, *get a copy for each of your adult and near-adult grandchildren, and maybe for your children, nieces and nephews, too.* Use it to open a dialogue about building wealth without getting too personal. If you get this as an eBook, consider getting print editions, too. Technology changes; print editions will be easier for your grandchildren to find and consult in future years.

My wish for you and your family is tremendous success!

Magical greetings,


Rich Hamilton
*Phoenix, Arizona*

**Books by Rich Hamilton:**

*Secret Wealth: A Financial Plan
to Share With Your Grandchildren*

*Disney Magic: Business Strategy
You Can Use at Work and at Home*

*Disney Magic Ideabook: Using Disney's Magic Strategy
for Your Own Business Success*

*Internet Business Magic: Using Disney's Magic Strategy
in Your Own Online Business*

**Internet Support:**

SecretWealth.com

# Table of Contents

# 1. A Letter to My Grandchildren about Wealth

This is a letter to you and each of my grandchildren.

I've printed it in book form so it will be easier for you to read, keep, and use for reference in coming years.

It is written with love and concern for your future.

My wish for you is that you enjoy a happy, successful life.

The nature of life tells us that there will be good times and bad, happy times and sad, times of depression, times of fear, times of joy, and times of satisfaction.

For most of us, having enough financial capability to live comfortably, cover a surprise car repair or home maintenance issue, and avoid financial worry is something to be happy about. Retiring without worry, being able to enjoy retirement, and knowing that you're retiring without becoming a financial burden on your children is something to be happy about. Having some money left over to pass on to your children or give to charities is something to be happy about.

---

*Wealth is security. It gives you the ability to take care of your needs without worry and without begging for help from others, or crying about what you need but can't have. That's something to be happy about.*

---

"While everyone is telling you to live it up in your 20s, plenty of your peers will also be (quietly) getting their finances in order," advises Heather Long in *CNNMoney*. "I really regret not opening an IRA (individual retirement account) and doing it myself. It's harder, but it's all about getting going early." (*CNNMoney,* "What I wish I knew about money on graduation day," May 26, 2015)

I've written this letter to you so you can be a *Wealth Builder* instead of a consumption focused *debt builder*. Building wealth is a lot more satisfying than building debt.

I wish I was writing this letter to tell you how smart I've been and how it's made me incredibly wealthy.

I've done some of it right and I've done some of it wrong. And much of it I did right some of the time. Looking back, I know I should have been doing that right stuff all the time. Reflecting, I know I could have done better. And I know you can do better, by using my 20-20 hindsight.

Learn from my successes, from my mistakes, and from the successes of people who have successfully built wealth.

Warren Buffett is one of the richest (and wisest) men in America, but if you meet him you'll think he's just a nice guy.

One of my cousins lived down the street from Buffett for several years and was aware of his reputation as a savvy investor. Was she clever enough to buy some of his Berkshire Hathaway stock? "No," Kathy sadly reports. "I sure wish I had!" Shares traded for $260 then, and that seemed expensive; now *the same shares* are over $200,000.

Buffett says, "In the business world, the rearview mirror is always clearer than the windshield." That's true here, too. My rearview mirror shows me clearly what I did right, and what I should have done differently.

I'll quote Buffett many times in this letter, but the plan I present is mine. I've learned a lot from him, and I've noticed that many of the things he says match up with my rearview mirror thinking.

Buffett is known as the "Oracle of Omaha." By age 14, Buffett had purchased a small farm near his hometown, Omaha, Nebraska, using profits from his paper route. By the time he graduated college, he had $90,000 in savings.

By 1962, Buffett was a millionaire with his investment partnership, and by 1990, he was a billionaire. Today, he's the second-richest man in America, just after Bill Gates.

He's frugal and charming. He seldom dines at expensive restaurants, preferring a local steakhouse in Omaha. He drives himself to work in a Cadillac that he's likely to keep for eight or more years. He's courteous and personable. And he often takes visitors to McDonald's on the way to the airport.

He freely shares practical investing advice with investors like you and me.

## 1.1.  Can You Reach Financial Independence at 39 Years Old?

"I'm 39, and my birthday is next week," the nurse at the hospital told me. "I'm retiring next week, because I can." If you've invested well, retirement doesn't have to mean waiting until you're 65 or 70 years old.

> *You may reach "financial independence" long before you reach retirement age. That's a good thing. It gives you options and choices.*

I'm going to talk a lot in this letter about retiring with wealth, but along the way you should reach a point of financial independence. Joe Udo defines *financial independence* as "having enough income to pay your living expenses for the rest of your life without having to work full time." (*US News & World Report,* Money blog, July 10, 2014)

Real financial independence means your money – your investments – are working for you, big enough and growing enough that you can draw your living expenses and still have enough of your investments left growing so you can expect your future withdrawals to increase, keeping up with inflation.

When you reach financial independence, you can choose when to stop working for wages.

Yes, retirement may come at 65 to 70 years old, or older, but it can also come sooner.

Or you may reach a time when you *could* retire early, but continue working by choice.

Financial independence will open up opportunities for travel, entertainment, and leisure.

Building wealth is about creating choices and opportunities, having your money work for you rather than you working for it, and having your money support you however long you live.

### 1.1.1.    I Wish I'd Had This Letter When I Was Starting Out

This is the letter I wish I'd had to plan my financial life at a young age. I think my dad, your great-grandfather Dick, would have liked to have it too. He did well, but there was no blueprint for him to make it easy; he had to design it as he lived it.

If I come back in another life I hope I find this book and take its advice to heart.

I'll try to keep this short, but it is a financial life plan and I don't think you'd want me to short you on that. It's more valuable than any inheritance I could leave you.

### 1.1.2.    I'm Sticking My Nose Where It Doesn't Belong

I don't think you should have to tell me about your finances, but I don't want to watch you struggle while I'm thinking, "I could have told them about that."

This letter is my answer, a collection of discussions we might have had, but you can take it or leave it. That's up to you.

This letter may seem critical of choices you may have made that don't fit this plan. That's not the intention. Nor is it intended to reflect on choices your parents or friends have made. Remember, much of this I learned by doing the wrong things, so if you think I'm pointing fingers, I'm pointing them at myself.

The magic here is common sense that gets ignored in the moments of leading a busy life. Being a Wealth Builder is remarkably easy and rewarding, but at times it means making tough, sometimes unpleasant, decisions.

Ultimately, you'll be happy as you make the decision to be a Wealth Builder.

### 1.1.3. *Is This a Long Letter?*

You may think this seems like a long letter, and it is. I'm sharing more than you need to know right now, but by reading it you'll be prepared when something comes up and you need it. That doesn't mean you'll remember it all; just hold on to the book so you can refer back to it as needed.

## 1.2. It's Your Choice

You can be a consumption focused *debt builder*.

Or you can be a *Wealth Builder*.

No one else can make the decision for you. No one else can get you to take the first step. No one else can get you to make the hard choices and the easy choices to build your future.

Not making a choice is a choice itself, and leaves you on the path to a consumption focused debt builder.

So I urge you to make the choice.

Building wealth is a lot more satisfying than building debt.

### 1.2.1. *A Word of Warning... and Why I Call This 'Secret Wealth'*

---

> *One of the wealthiest men I've known told me he was often asked for information about his business or about his wealth.*
> *"I just tell them, 'That's a secret,' and it's the end of it."*

---

If you tell anyone you have investments, one of two things is likely to happen.

First, they may start telling you about their own investments and how smart they are investing in this or that, or why they like junk bonds, or giving you some stock tip, or some other idea. Most of these ideas are crazy; a few might have merit. But I urge you to ignore them. It will just confuse your own investment plan.

Second, they may either think you have a lot of money, or they will resent your apparent situation and it will become a barrier in your relationship. They may even decide you should loan them some money or join them as a partner in their purchase of a boat, airplane, or some other consumption oriented idea.

It's better that you keep your plans a secret.

What if you have a good friend who seems to want a way to invest or put aside savings?

If you want you could tell him your Granddaddy shared a few ideas and tell him how to get a copy of this book. Don't give him your copy, don't buy one for him, and don't make a big deal about it. If he really cares, he will invest in his own copy. And later, if he asks how you're doing with it, stay cool and give no details. Just shrug, and mumble, "Yeah, well you know how things go."

It's your secret; it's no one else's business. That won't keep them from asking, but you don't have to tell. Just say, "Sorry, that's a secret."

## 1.3.    What's Ahead?

This letter is divided into several parts:

1. Being wealthy and how to become a Wealth Builder.

2. The plan for financial success and an understanding of credit.

It's about getting a job and investing a portion of your income and letting it grow to build wealth. I'll also discuss how much you'll need when you retire – it's more than you thought!

3. Investing, including two easy-to-use strategies.

Strategy A is the easiest plan and will return a handsome profit, allowing you to build wealth.

Strategy B offers an opportunity to grow your wealth considerably more than Strategy A in return for taking more risk. It also requires a time investment for a bit of research and thinking, but I'll share with you exactly how to go about that. It's nearly as easy as Strategy A, and I consider it the better approach.

4. Living life as a Wealth Builder, including advice about how to retire.

5. How to get started, including step-by-step instructions and a section on what to do if you're so far in debt you think you can't get started.

Becoming a Wealth Builder involves investing and there's always some risk in that. I firmly believe these strategies will minimize your risk.

# 2. About Being Wealthy

BEING WEALTHY ISN'T WHAT YOU THINK!

Your *mindset* is a pretty important thing; the mindset is the set of assumptions, methods, or beliefs that is so strong is becomes the basis for your actions. It may also be described as your philosophy of life.

What really separates the wealthy from the rest of us?

"Their beliefs around money, success, achievement and everything connected to compensation and amassing wealth," according to Steve Siebold, author of *How Rich People Think*.

That's why this letter is about more than an investment plan; we're going to start by exploring wealth including what wealth looks like, how much you will need, and when you should start working on it. I'll share a story about a Personal Balance Sheet and how to build one.

---

*Since wages from a job generate the cash that you invest as well as the money you spend, it's pretty important that you have a good job.*

---

I'll spend some time sharing what I learned about job hunting when I was an employer as well as when I was looking for work.

You are not your job. Your job is something you do.

When I was younger I got mixed up about who I was, and it was always about what job I was doing. When I was in radio broadcasting, I thought I had to do radio "because *that's who I am.*" Later, when I worked as a computer systems analyst, I thought *that* was who I had become.

I saw an episode of *The Mentalist* where Patrick Jane was talking to Teresa Lisbon about quitting the FBI. "I can't quit," she protested. "It's who I am." That's just wrong.

Your job is what you do. It shouldn't be what you do forever. Your job is not who you are.

Andrew Carnegie was a 19th century industrialist who led the expansion of the American steel industry. But steel was not who he was. After he sold his steel company, he devoted his life to philanthropy, especially local libraries, world peace, education and scientific research.

Jimmy Carter served as the President of the United States from 1977 to 1981. But being president is what he did, not who he is. Since leaving the White House, he has conducted peace negotiations, observed elections, and advanced disease prevention and eradication in developing nations. He has been active in Habitat for Humanity, even helping to construct homes.

Bill Gates is a computer programmer and inventor who co-founded Microsoft. But that's what he did, not who he is. Today Gates and his wife, Melinda, focus on enhancing healthcare and reducing extreme poverty around the world, and on expanding educational opportunities and increasing access to information technology in the United States.

---

*You are not your job. Your job is something you do.*

---

Having enough money when you decide to retire gives you the freedom to do the things that make you whole. What makes you whole doesn't have to be as grand as Carnegie, Carter, or Gates. It just has to be right for you.

*Not* having enough money means you *have* to sit at home and watch TV.

## 2.1. People Who Wish They Were Broke

The average American is broke and buying things they cannot afford with credit cards and other debt, putting them below broke!

That's most people. In the United States most households carry too much credit. On average, each household with a credit card carries card debt of $15,191, resulting in interest payments of $3,200 or more per year.

These people can't afford that $3,200 credit card interest payment.

Add car loans, student loans, home loans, home equity loans, and other loans and you punch that average up to $117,951. The average mortgage debt is $154,365. The average student loan debt is $33,607.

According to Experian Automotive (on CNBC March 4, 2014, by Phil LeBeau), the average auto loan for a new car is $27,430. The average used car loan is $17,974.

As loans rise, finding a low monthly payment is harder, resulting in extended payback times and bigger interest bills. The average monthly payment for a new car auto loan is $471; used car loan payments average $352.

According to Experian, 20 percent of all new car auto loans are now more than six years in length.

By the time you read this these numbers will probably be even higher.

All these debts put people "in the hole," owing so much they wish they could just be broke. Instead, they're below broke.

That's about average Americans.

You don't want to be an average broke American, do you?

It's easy to say that credit card debt accounts for the majority of the debt Americans have today. However, it is in fact the *third* biggest source of debt for U.S. households, following student loans and mortgage loans.

Forty percent of Americans don't save *anything* for retirement. A majority of Americans have invested *nothing* in the stock market. That's *their* fault!

Most of the people you think are wealthy are just deep in debt; they've bought all the "stuff" and ended up with lots of payments with little hope of paying it all off.

## 2.2.  Get-Rich-Quick Schemes

Ever get offered an opportunity to gain your financial freedom? Whether it's a home study course advertised on late night TV for getting rich buying real estate, a business opportunity, a "hot" stock tip, collectibles, or just popping for lottery tickets at the convenience store, the odds are severely against you anytime making money seems too easy to be true.

I had a software client in Louisiana who actually did make money by following one of those TV real estate plans, even appearing on their TV infomercials. He told me about it as he was nearing his 90th birthday. "I was incredibly lucky to be doing this in the right community at the right time, he told me. "I really doubt others will find much success." He confided, "This takes a lot of time. It's becoming much more difficult to manage these rentals and I'm having trouble selling properties. It's hard work!"

The Wealth Builder plan I'm sharing with you here is much better than that.

## 2.3.  Collectibles are Questionable as Investments

A friend died recently in Kansas, leaving his wife with the task of selling the huge collection of fine art and collectibles they had put together during their successful lives together. Those collectibles had a high value, and comprised much of their wealth. "It's incredibly hard," she told me, "to find buyers for *all* this stuff."

The Wealth Builder plan I'm sharing with you here focuses on *liquidity*, which means it can be turned to cash almost instantly. Collectibles, along with real estate investments and owning a small business, don't offer much liquidity. Even though this letter is about investing to build wealth for the long term, the day will come when you want to cash in, quickly and easily.

## 2.4. How to Build Wealth

### 2.4.1. *Start Now*

Time is the biggest secret.

When you're young you think you have a whole long lifetime ahead of you. And you're right.

The secret is to take advantage of that time instead of frittering it away.

Most people put it off, hoping to get around to building a little wealth when they're making a bit more money. It never happens.

Warren Buffett said, "Someone's sitting in the shade today because someone planted a tree a long time ago."

---

*The magic secret which I will reveal precisely in the coming pages is that by taking action now and using time profitably you can let time do most of the work for you as you build wealth.*

---

In a few pages I'm going to show you how spending $1,000 on something today will cost you $176,000 later.

I'll also show you how to turn $1,000 into $176,000, with very little work.

That is real magic!

### 2.4.2. *But It's Never Too Late to Start*

While time is a magic potion for building wealth, it's never too late.

Please don't take this as an excuse to wait. But if your parents or in-laws pick up this book, they can still build a lot of wealth to add on to what they already have.

I've already admitted that I wish I'd done things differently.

I started my investment program when I was 35 years old. I got into a discussion with Paul Brown, a Colorado business associate, and we each started an investment program similar to what I'm going to describe here. I wish I'd started 10 or 15 years earlier, but I know I can't let regrets get in the way of doing what needs to get done. After I started, I made plenty of mistakes.

I want you to know that I'm actively doing what I can, even at my current age, to be a Wealth Builder. I may not be able to turn $1,000 into $176,000 like I'll show you later because I don't have as much time as you. But I can turn $500 a month into $123,000 in 10 years. Knowing that, I can be motivated to live a Wealth Builder lifestyle.

## 2.5. What Is Wealth?

Dad told me a story about when he was a Navy airman during World War II. One day at mail call one of his buddies received a check in the mail. It was a dividend check, paid by a company whose stock his buddy owned.

"You mean you got a check and didn't have to work for it?" Dad asked.

"Right," came the reply, "I took money I earned, bought shares in the company, and now they send me checks. Because I own part of the company, a tiny part, they send me my share of the profits."

That's where Dad first learned about investing. It's the core idea of building wealth, money you get but don't have to work for. "I'd always had to work a job to get money," Dad told me. "For me, this was a new idea."

### 2.5.1. *Wages Pay Your Living, But Don't Build Wealth*

Earning wages in a job is a good thing. That's how we pay our living expenses, right? We use the money we earn at a job. We also use wages as a source of money to invest.

Very few people will ever earn enough to be wealthy because they will spend all they earn. In fact, they will overspend by using credit and then struggle just to "catch up" to broke.

Sure, there are a tiny few... sports figures and movie stars... who suddenly get big paychecks and manage not to blow the money as fast as they earn it, but most of those will find themselves broke a few years after the paychecks end.

## 2.6. Is Wealth Money?

There are many kinds of wealth. There is wealth in the friends you know, in your family relationships, in having a loving spouse and in having children. There is wealth in self-reliance, good health, longevity, and happiness. There is wealth in having a good reputation, honesty, respect, integrity, and a history of achievement.

This letter is not about that kind of wealth, but learning about "money wealth" will teach you principles that will pay off in "relationships wealth" and "family love wealth."

I think that's because creating "money wealth" requires a plan, discipline, and a responsibility toward your future and well-being, and those behaviors apply to living a full and rewarding life.

This is about a lifestyle that will lead you to wealth. Rather than "looking wealthy" you will actually be wealthy.

"Of the billionaires I have known," Warren Buffett says, "money just brings out the basic traits in them. If they were jerks before they had money, they are simply jerks with a billion dollars."

### 2.6.1.  Does having wealth make you happier?

People in richer countries are, on average, more satisfied with their lives according to Justin Wolfers, professor of Economics and Public Policy, University of Michigan (*Money*, June, 2014).

Within individual countries feelings of well-being grow as earnings grow. Wolfers says this may not be a direct correlation between money and happiness, but wealth seems to make the environment for satisfaction better.

### 2.6.2.  It's Not How Much You Get, It's How Much You Keep

Jerry Fitch told me once, "It's not about how much you get, it's about how much you keep." As a Durango, Colo., broadcaster, he was talking about running a radio station, but I learned that the most important business you can run is your household, your family.

### 2.6.3.  Is it About Being 'Tight?'

Not really.

Whatever your income, always live below your means. I prefer to think of it as being frugal.

---

*Building wealth is about knowing which money you can spend
and which not to spend.*

---

Most of the wealthy in the United States do not live in Beverly Hills or on Park Avenue. According to *The Millionaire Next Door* (Gallery Books, 1998) by Thomas J Stanley, Ph.D., and William D. Danko, Ph.D., the wealthy live right in your neighborhood. They shop for bargain-priced used cars, rear children who are unaware of their wealth, and reject a lifestyle of flashy exhibitionism and consumption.

Most of the people we think of as "rich" are deep in debt, putting on a show of glamour, according to Stanley and Danko. They take the money they earn and spend it, then spend more by using credit cards and borrowing money. These people have no idea how they will handle retirement.

Yes, a tiny few celebrities, sports figures, and business tycoons earn a lot and spend lavishly.

But most Wealth Builders are down-to-earth, frugal people who manage their wealth quietly and soundly, living below their means.

## 2.7.   I Went to See the Banker

Today I don't even remember why I wanted to borrow the money, but I went to the bank to see about getting a loan. Actually, I went to more than one bank. All turned me down.

One was special.

A small town banker, Glenn Watmore, turned me down but had a visit with me about my Personal Balance Sheet. I didn't really know what a Personal Balance Sheet was, but I graduated college with a Bachelor's of Business Administration and I knew what a *business* Balance Sheet was. I learned that a Personal Balance Sheet was the same thing, applied to my household rather than a company. It listed my assets like cars, homes, and household goods, plus any investments. And it listed my liabilities, which was everything I owed. The difference was my personal net worth.

Since I owed less than I owned in assets, I had a positive net worth. But it wasn't much.

Glenn told me I needed to work on my balance sheet and *build a substantial net worth*.

Over the years he became a friend. He never intruded, but showed me a few things, mostly by example, that I could do to build my net worth.

His bank loaned me money to buy a house, and he taught me to maintain a substantial liquid capitalization, which means to have a lot more liquid assets (like cash or investments that can be quickly sold for cash) than I owe.

Dad was trying to teach me those same things, but, like many sons, I was slow to pay attention. It took awhile for it to sink in; eventually I got it.

## 2.8.   Understand Your Personal Balance Sheet and Your Net Worth

To be a Wealth Builder you need to manage your personal cash flow so you have a surplus of money that can be used to build your net worth.

First calculate your net worth by laying out a personal balance sheet. That's what the banker asked me about. It's really pretty easy to do. In the Appendix of this book I'm including a blank form you can copy and use to create your own personal balance sheet. Then you can update this periodically – every month, every few months, or every year.

Here's what you'll find on your personal balance sheet:

**Long-Term Assets**. These are things you own that would take some time to sell if you needed to sell to get cash. This will include things like your home (if you own it), automobiles, furniture, household goods, and recreational equipment. You should also include retirement accounts (IRA and 401-K accounts) that shouldn't be cashed out until you retire.

Appendix    Personal Balance Sheet

**ASSETS**

Long-Term Assets

| 2008 Ford Focus | $5160.00 |
| Furniture & Household Goods | $500.00 |
| Roth IRA Retirement Account | $14610.05 |
| Total Long-Term Assets | $20,270.05 |

Liquid Assets

| Wealth Builder Account | $14610.05 |
| Protection Account | $1222.05 |
| Checking Balance | $465.17 |
| Total Liquid Assets | $27,296.27 |
| TOTAL ASSETS (Long-Term Assets + Liquid Assets) | $47,566.32 |

**LIABILITIES**

| Auto Loan | $3280.00 |
| Credit Card | $127.00 |
| | $ |
| | $ |
| TOTAL LIABILITIES | $3407.00 |

**NET WORTH** (Total Assets – Total Liabilities)    $44,159.32

**Liquid Assets**. This is everything else you own that you can convert to cash within five days. This will include cash, stocks, and mutual funds that you can cash out quickly on the market. (If you own securities that can't be cashed out within five days, including restricted stocks or stocks of small businesses that are not traded on the market, they should be listed under long-term assets.)

**Total Assets**. This is the sum of all long-term and liquid assets.

**Liabilities**. This is everything you owe, including credit cards, home mortgages, car loans, store credit, medical bills, loans from friends or family... everything you owe.

**Net Worth**. Take total assets and subtract total liabilities. That's your net worth.

### 2.8.1.  What Values to Put on Your Assets?

When listing your assets you should list values as *real market values*, not what you paid for something. That takes some guessing, especially on things like your home and automobiles, but you may get help from websites like zillow.com and edmunds.com. The values for household goods, tools, and recreational equipment will be shockingly low; price them below garage sale prices here; remember that when you have a garage sale not everything sells.

The value of most things people buy goes down immediately, and it's a fast decline. Sorry... that's just how it is. Your goal is to show yourself the actual value of your current estate, so it does no good to inflate values.

### 2.8.2.  Your Personal Cash Flow (Spending Plan)

After calculating your personal net worth, you want to lay out your cash flow. Your personal cash flow statement is really your spending plan, and we'll get into that later. For now, you need to get ready to list your income, your investment plan, and your expenses. In the Appendix of this book I'm including a blank form you can copy and use to create your own Personal Cash Flow (Spending Plan).

This will be the key to your financial strategy.

Accumulating money is not your ultimate goal. Ultimately you want to spend money. Done right, you will accumulate money and let that accumulated money work for you; eventually you'll spend a portion of the money it generates on the things that fit with your values and desires. That's what building wealth is about.

## 2.9. How Much Do You Need Per Year?

When I started working in the late 1960s folks who made $10,000 weren't super rich by any means, but the $10,000 mark indicated a higher than normal income. (It was not quite twice the median household income in 1967.)

Forty years later as I neared retirement, it took a $100,000 annual income to fit that description. ($100,000 is not quite twice the current median household income in the United States.)

*I don't want to suggest that this is the correct amount for you. It's just a nice round amount for you to think about as you make your own financial plan. You might think the annual income should be $60,000... or $400,000. You have to establish your own objectives, and you need to be able to adapt as life's challenges and opportunities change your perspective. That's all up to you.*

---

*The number is relative to when you start. But forty years of inflation and growth will probably mean that whatever you think is good money today will have become ten times that amount when you retire.*

---

I'm going to minimize use of the term *millionaire* in this letter because today's income of $100,000 will be $1,000,000 in forty years after factoring in inflation. That's right, if you're just starting in the workforce today, when you retire lots of people will be making a million bucks a year! They will be doing well, and will be millionaires. But they won't be wealthy.

A *decamillionaire* is someone with a net worth of ten million dollars or more. A *hectomillionaire* is someone with a net worth of one hundred million dollars or more.

Due to inflation, when you retire forty or more years from now you'll want to be a decamillionaire or hectomillionaire, or somewhere in that range. Today that sounds crazy. But in forty years, it will make sense. And it's possible!

A proper wealth strategy will prepare you to have enough to retire handsomely and to have wealth to pass on to your family. And, yes, along the way you will lead a more than comfortable life.

Earlier I said I'm going to show you how spending $1,000 on something today will cost you $176,000 later. Part of the secret is knowing that later it will take $10,000 to buy that $1,000 thing, but also knowing that having $176,000 means you'll have $166,000 extra because you followed a wealth strategy.

This sounds like magic, and it is! But it's real magic that you can perform throughout your life.

### 2.9.1.   How much will you need when you retire?

A financial writer recently suggested you should be debt-free before you retire.

Many financial advisors suggest you need 75% of your pre-retirement income when you retire.

While I agree with both of these ideas, it's not nearly good enough.

Can you count on Social Security? Politicians keep reminding us that the Social Security fund is in trouble. (It's because they have tapped it for other things.) Since it is politics I expect there will be something like Social Security available when you retire.

But will it do the job? No. "Social Security benefits are not intended to be your only income source when you retire," says the Social Security Administration. "You will need other savings, investments, pensions, or retirement accounts to live comfortably." (*Social Security Statement*, Jan. 2, 2015) Social Security amounts to keeping your granddaddy and others his age at a level barely above the poverty line.

What about your company's 401-K or pension plan? Add it to Social Security and it may cover your basic expenses. But it won't repair your car, and certainly won't buy you a new one. It won't fund a nice vacation.

I hope your home will be paid for by then because what you get from Social Security won't cover much rent.

### 2.9.2.   Why You Need More to Retire than Before Retirement

I calculated once how much I needed when I retire.

I will need more than when I was working because I will have more time to do things. Retirement need not – should not –  mean sitting at home watching TV.

I will want to maintain my investments and live on the income from those investments rather than depleting the principal investment.

I want to have enough to move to a retirement home when the time is right and to maintain myself so I am not a burden to my family.

For planning purposes, if I think I need $100,000 a year when I retire, it means I need to have invested 2.5 million dollars in a way that I can draw 4% annually. The calculation? Four percent of 2.5 million dollars is $100,000.

You? You'll need ten times that to allow for 40 or 50 years of inflation. That's 25 million dollars. Do you have your plan ready to accomplish that?

*I know that sounds incredible, but if you hold on to this letter in 40 years you'll be astounded at how much smaller 25 million seems then. If you've followed these suggestions, I think you'll be well prepared.*

## 2.10. It's Not About Flash

By the way, most of the people you see with big homes and fancy cars are *not wealthy*, but they're excited about *looking wealthy*. That is not financial health. Fancy homes and expensive cars usually mean big mortgages and car payments. They've probably borrowed to the max on credit cards and store credit to afford fancy furniture, extravagant vacations, and expensive jewelry.

When these folks lose a job through downsizing or get hit with an unexpected medical bill, they're in trouble, scrambling to borrow more just to get by.

## 2.11. Secret Wealth

There's a really nice guy in my area who is retired and well-invested. He tells me, "Rich, I can't believe what I've done. I invested in a few mutual funds and left them alone. The stock market has been good to me. I've given over a million dollars to each of my children and still have about twelve million left. I can do what I want and the kids will inherit a lot."

This guy lives in a modest home in a decent neighborhood. He travels several times a year, drives a nice, intermediate size, domestic car, and looks like most of my other neighbors.

There's no flash in his life, yet I'm sure he has everything he needs or wants. If his car breaks down he gets it fixed or replaced; there's no trauma. If the air conditioner gives him trouble, he gets it fixed. He delights in getting a good deal just like everyone else.

He's done better than others because he decided to invest and became a Wealth Builder.

No one else in the neighborhood knows how well he has done. And it's none of their business.

### 2.11.1. *Keep your Wealth a Secret*

As you build wealth, it may be enticing to share your successes with friends and associates.

It's better to keep it a secret. Live in a modest home, drive a modest car, and wear "real people" clothes. But don't look like a bum.

If you want a nice car (and can afford it) get a modest car with all the options. A Buick with all options can be nearly as luxurious as a Cadillac, but it "looks" less pretentious. (We'll talk more about buying a car later.)

If people think you're wealthy:

You will get lots of requests for "loans" and "gifts."

You make yourself a target for thieves.

You become a target for investment advisors and stock brokers who have the "very best" investments for you. (They don't.)

You will create animosity among your friends and associates.

People you work with (and especially anyone who works for you) will think you're "made of money" and think they should be paid more.

Your neighbors will resent you.

If you buy a "too fancy" house or car, it's just the same as bragging to your "not so well off" friends about how well you're doing. And no one likes a braggart.

It's not a pretty picture. So keep it a secret.

Keeping it a secret includes both the things you talk about and the things you do.

Think about it. If you have someone coming to bid a job at your home fixing the roof and you meet them driving up in your Cadillac, Mercedes, or Rolls-Royce, do you really think you'll get the same bid price as if they met you driving up in a Ford or Volkswagen?

Never tell your children their parents are wealthy. Teach them responsibility, discipline, and frugality. Teach them about working hard, saving, investing, and liquidity. The last thing you need is your children bragging to their friends, "My dad has more money than your dad!"

Don't try to compete with your children, your relatives, or your friends. Never boast about how much you have accumulated.

A common thought should be:

*"People would be astonished at how much wealth I have accumulated. I know how to hang on to it."*

## 2.12. How to be a Wealth Builder

When I was 21 I remember visiting another married couple who were moving to a rental home from a furnished apartment. I accompanied them on a trip to Sears where they shopped for laundry appliances.

They found the equipment they wanted and the salesman quoted them the "additional monthly payment" that would be added to their existing Sears payment plan. I learned that they had already purchased furniture on payments from Sears.

They paid very little attention to the cost of the appliances or the interest they would pay; they were only interested in the payment and whether they could squeeze the payment into their meager budget.

They were well on the road to building debt.

Another couple I knew were moving into a rental house and they, too, needed laundry equipment and furniture.

They made a game of finding what they wanted at extremely low prices at garage sales, and negotiating the prices even lower.

They fit the "payments" into their budget, too, but there were no ongoing monthly payments. Some of their furniture was a bit worn, but most looked like new.

Today, in addition to garage sales, there are flea markets, stores like Goodwill and Savers, warehouse stores, and online sources like Craig's List and eBay that make it possible to shop for real bargains. It takes a bit of work and patience, but there really are ways to get equipped as you need to and still be frugal.

---

*Building wealth takes sacrifice, discipline, and hard work, qualities that are positively discouraged by our high-consumption society. It's your choice; make it a positive decision in your favor.*

---

## 2.13. Three Kinds of People

Most people fall into one of three groups when it comes to how they manage their finances.

### 1. Month to Month, or Check to Check

Most people live today for today, getting by on what they make, and getting into financial pickles time after time. They have no effective financial plan, spend money as they get it, and use credit cards and store credit to buy what they want. As a result they are in debt.

As of this writing, the average household credit card debt in the United States was $15,191 resulting in interest payments of $3,000 or more per year.

They probably drive cars they can't afford; enjoy fancy electronics, jewelry, and clothing; and live in a home that's beyond their means, all financed with credit.

They often need help affording expenses such as loss of employment, college expenses for a child, and out of pocket medical expenses.

Money is a constant challenge.

About one-fourth of Americans have no emergency savings according to a study by Greg McBride, chief financial analyst at Bankrate.com, reported in *USA Today* June 23, 2014.

"If you don't have emergency savings, what do you do when you have an unplanned expense or the money runs out before the bills do?" McBride asks. "You're stuck. That means for some people (turning to) high-cost borrowing, check cashing, a payday lender."

McBride says Americans tend to buy too much stuff.

"I've had people stand in front of me with a $5 latte and a $500 iPad and say they couldn't possibly save more than they are now," he says.

## 2. *Month to Month, But a Home Investment*

These folks are not much different but they have invested in buying a home.

If they chose their home wisely, avoid second mortgages, and pay it off early, they will have a valuable asset and avoid paying rent.

## 3. *Wealth Builders*

This is a relatively small group of people, but you probably know some right in your own neighborhood. You may not know how well they're doing because they don't talk about it and they live modestly.

That same *USA Today* story told about 30-year old Jeremy Roberts who says he and his wife Charity decided to start living "off much less than we make... We started living in smaller places, driving older vehicles, and saving more money." He claims, "It has resulted in both financial freedom and it makes our marriage better."

## *Instant Wealth*

There *is* a fourth category I call the "Lucky Few." These are folks who find instant wealth through inheritance, lottery winnings, or having a job where their company experiences huge growth and they profit through stock options or other distributions. A few celebrities and sports figures also experience windfall incomes.

Frankly, most of these folks never learned about wealth building so they splurge away their instant wealth.

# 2.14. 'Pay Yourself First'

When I was young, banks would advertise, "Pay yourself first."

They were trying to get people to save money in savings accounts paying very low interest. The concept is sound. You just want to earn considerably more than a bank's interest rate.

The idea was that each time you received a paycheck, a portion of that should be put into savings *before* applying the rest to living your life.

---

*A part of all you earn is yours to keep. Most of your wages go to pay for clothes, food, rent, etc., but if you regularly save a portion of your wages and put that money to work by investing and reinvesting the profits from your investments, you will become wealthy.*

---

## 2.15. Get a Good Job

Does it surprise you that I'm going to talk about getting a good job? It shouldn't, since wages from a job fund your wealth building.

You may start as a cook or crew chief at McDonalds, but unless you move into management (with better pay, bonuses, health benefits and a retirement plan) pretty fast, you should be looking for something better.

Choose your occupation wisely.

It's been said that you should do something you love. I agree with that, but I will extend it a bit:

*Do something you love enough... and that you do well... that will pay you handsomely over your lifetime.*

If you love sitting on the beach or partying at a night club, that probably won't pay you well over your lifetime.

But if you love going to Disneyland consider getting a job at Disneyland with an eye toward management, project management, or creative management. You may have to start in an entry level job, but plan from the beginning how you may move to a better position. Tony Baxter started as a teenager selling popcorn in front of Sleeping Beauty castle and retired as vice-president of Imagineering.

Maybe you could be a writer for a newspaper and cover entertainment, or write for an entertainment magazine. These could have you reporting on news at Disneyland and other venues.

Chris, a Phoenix-area friend, moved to California and used his college degree and considerable experience in the automobile business to land a well-paying job at Disneyland. No entry-level jobs for Chris! But he had to gain experience outside that would translate to valuable skills inside Disneyland.

### 2.15.1. What is a Good Job?

A good job is a job with good pay, good promotion opportunities, and benefits.

By benefits I mean:

**Healthcare**. A few top companies pay all healthcare costs for you and your family. Most pay your cost and part of your family premium.

**Retirement Plan**. A pension or 401-K retirement plan means you contribute toward your retirement and your employer matches it up to a point. You want to maximize that and get the maximum employer contribution.

If a job doesn't give you a good healthcare plan, at least some kind of retirement plan, and growth opportunity it should be considered a temporary job.

**Growth Opportunity**. You should expect cost-of-living raises plus merit raises and/or promotion opportunities. (Otherwise it's known as a *dead-end job*.)

**Is a commission sales job a good job?** Maybe. When Karen sold cars she made good money, but the hours were long. The key question is: Can *you* consistently earn good money at this commission job? Some people thrive in this environment. It sounds easy, but *most do not*.

I remember a year in Durango, Colorado, where there were many more "active" real estate salespeople than there were homes sold that year. That means most of those salespeople made nothing, while just a few did very well. Not good.

## 2.15.2. *Better yet, get two jobs*

When Jay Leno retired after 20-some years of hosting the Tonight show, he revealed a secret. Leno didn't spend any of what he earned from the show, as much as $15 million annually in the final years. He continued to live off the income from his standup comedy act.

"When I was a kid, I had two jobs," Leno wrote in Parade magazine. "I worked at a Ford dealership and at a McDonald's. I'd spend the money from one job and save the money from the other. That's still the way I am now."

So... you can work a second job yourself. Or, maybe...

## 2.15.3. *If Married, Should You Both Work?*

The *financial* answer to this is a resounding "Yes!"

Why? Because it doubles the potential income for you to invest and spend.

If you're married, you can both work, and the added income can mean you live better, invest more, and build your protection fund faster.

This is a choice, and it's not right for everyone. When you have a family, managing the family and household takes a lot of time and attention. Not taking advantage of a second income costs you a lot of money, but if your main income is enough and the benefits are adequate, you may decide a second income is not required.

Just be sure you know that you're missing out on a significant investible income. It's your decision.

## 2.16.  What to Do While You're Looking for a Good Job

Get a less-good job to help with cash flow, and continue the job search.

Sometimes the lesser job turns into a good job. Clerking at the grocery store will get you by but it could also get you into a management position with a potential for better pay and benefits.

## 2.17.  You're *Always* Looking for a Job

The days of job security are gone. Fifty or a hundred years ago you might take a job and continue working for that company until you retired. That hardly ever happens today. Even after you land a good job, keep looking for a better job.

Look for other jobs inside your company and look at other companies.

Do it by building networks of people you know in the company and outside. Attend meetings and vocational group gatherings in your own and in other fields. Go to the local meetings. Volunteer for their projects.

Participate in business forums online.

Get out of the regular workplace. Volunteer to represent your company at conferences and conventions and appear on panels.

If your company doesn't want to sponsor you going to these meetings, pay your own way. It will help you in your current job and may help you when you need a new one.

### 2.17.1.  *Be a Moneymaker*

If prospects for a promotion are lacking, watch for another job in the same company that is closer to sales and marketing.

When I was working in a government job, I learned that working for the IT department wasn't as good as working a special IT position in asset sales. In fact, sales and marketing departments often hire specialists of their own, and fit it into *their* budgets, not the IT department's budgets. Departments that bring money in are often better paid.

## 2.18.  To Get and Keep a Good Job, *Always* Look and Act the Part

Not long ago I was at a nice dinner where the hostess repeatedly talked while she was chewing her food. We've all witnessed these gaffes from time to time where someone either doesn't know better manners, or they don't care.

> *How many bright, knowledgeable people fail because they lack the social graces? Management theorist Peter Drucker called manners the "lubricating oil" of an organization. It matters.*

### 2.18.1. *A Chance Encounter Paid Off 15 Years Later*

My first visit to a Disney theme park was in 1986 following a photography conference in Miami. Two other photographers and their spouses joined me after the conference to tour Walt Disney World. Over the years we exchanged a few Christmas cards.

Fifteen years later I sent Christmas cards with a Christmas letter including a note that "If you know any meeting planners tell them about my new *Disney Magic* book and that I speak about Disney success secrets."

Though we had not talked in years Claudia, one of those photographers I met in 1986, called, saying, *"I'm a meeting planner now* and maybe we can get you in as one of our programs." She did, and it was the first of several speaking engagements with that firm.

Remember, Claudia didn't know me as a writer, a speaker, or even a Disney expert. She was there when I *first* went to a Disney theme park. But 15 years later she had the confidence to hire me as an expert speaker because I made a good impression.

### 2.18.2. *A Small Meal at McDonalds Led to a Job Months Later*

I met Rick at a computer users group. We exchanged the typical friendly hellos, and visited lightly during breaks. One Saturday morning we each attended a training session conducted by the users group.

After the training, several of us sat down at an outdoor table and discussed the training. It was a hot day in Arizona, so Rick suggested we move to a nearby McDonalds, where I shared with the others some strategies for using the tool discussed in the training.

Several months later, I received an email to call Rick. He was a department manager, needed to hire some people, and hoped I would submit an application. I did, and I was hired for a responsible position.

If I had taken that casual lunch at McDonalds and shown the casual manners that we often see people use at fast food restaurants, do you think I would have landed that position? I doubt it. Even at McDonald's, it matters.

In both of these situations, I was not seeking employment; I was networking with people of common interests. By making a good impression, job opportunities followed.

Will they always? No. But by planting enough of those good impressions, there will be opportunities. We make our own good luck.

### 2.18.3. Sharing Pizza for Lunch

When Ken Willard was in radio station management in Kansas, he shared a hiring technique. After interviewing a job applicant, if the applicant seemed promising, he would offer to buy lunch and they would go to Pizza Hut where they would share a pizza.

He told me the applicant often let his guard down over a shared pizza.

It gave Ken an opportunity to evaluate the applicant in a social situation and Ken could reinforce his initial opinion or... change it.

Ken wanted to hire someone who would make a great impression, not someone who would embarrass the station at work or in the community.

### 2.18.4. In Your Daily Work, Look Like Your Next Promotion

"Dress for success" is a phrase you hear bandied about; what it means is that every day you need to look and act like you're at a job interview for your boss's job... or her boss's job.

That means clothes, grooming, and behavior. If you go to lunch with coworkers smile, and participate in the conversation. Never bad-mouth the company, even in agreement with what others say... and even if you think the criticism is correct.

---

*Dad always told me to "Never burn bridges." He meant that you never know where your next job or referral might come from, so always make a good impression. And never do anything to sour that impression.*

---

Some of the people where you want to work might have prejudices against some facial hair, hairstyles, or tattoos; think about the impression you'll make and tone it down or hide tattoos for work situations.

You might think I mean you should "dress up" in coat and tie for men or corresponding work-appropriate dress for women. Maybe, but that depends on the culture of where you are working or want to work.

When I worked at FDIC we wore banking attire, suit and tie, but I worked with other programmers who in previous work at Intel had worn jeans and t-shirts to work. Again, look up to your boss's boss and see what's worn. You want to be headed in that direction, and you want to make a good impression when you get an unexpected meeting with higher management.

In the Art and Creative departments at Disney appearances are much more relaxed and expressive than they are in Disney corporate management. If you're at a company like Disney and have your sights set on management, you'd better look the part. Again, use my advice about dressing and looking like your boss's boss.

I met a guy at a Disneyana function who probably has more tattoos than anyone you've ever seen (and they're all Disney tattoos). He works at a bank. But he likes tattoos. So he gets his tattoos placed where they are hidden by his work clothes and cannot be seen by customers or coworkers.

At Disney they teach their cast members that in many cultures it is rude to point with one finger. Pointing at someone can be rude, and even pointing down the street with one finger can make a negative impression. It's true in many countries and in many circles in the United States.

It's often necessary to point when giving directions. So Disney teaches that you point with two fingers, or with your whole hand. It's a simple solution.

I had an employee once whose car had a funny bumper sticker that read, "My boss is a pig." I'm pretty sure that bumper sticker was in place before she started working for me, but what will folks think about doing business with my company when they see that bumper sticker on her car? Might that affect how I think about promoting her or giving a raise?

All these things speak about you and can affect your income.

### 2.18.5. *You're Seen in Social Media, Too*

It's easy to forget all about work when you're posting in social media but those posts are public (or nearly so) and can be read by employers and potential employers, sometimes years later. Even your choice of friends and the things they post can affect the way someone sees you.

---

*Don't think your postings in social media are private; even privacy settings may not protect you. Lots of people have lost jobs or failed to get a job because of what they posted in social media.*

---

After 11 years as the voice of the Aflac duck, actor and comedian Gilbert Gottfried was fired after tweeting jokes about the earthquake and tsunami in Japan.

Nicole Crowther was a recurring extra on Glee, fired after she tweeted some plot spoilers she had heard on set.

Former MLB pitcher Mike Bacsik lost his radio job after tweeting some racially-loaded comments during a Mavericks-Spurs game.

A 22-year-old North Carolina waitress blasted two customers on Facebook for stiffing her on the tip. She was fired for breaking a rule about disparaging the customers.

A Bronx high school teacher was fired for posting "This is sexy" under pictures students shared on Facebook.

Is this fair? That's immaterial. Be careful what you say.

### 2.18.6. *Language Mistakes that Mark You as Less Intelligent than You Are*

There are certain common phrases that are incorrect uses of English and will mark you as less intelligent than you probably are. Here are several things you should never say:

1. "Her and I are going to..." *Instead, say: "She and I are..."*
2. "He don't care about me anymore." *Instead: "He doesn't care..."*
3. "I'm not speaking to nobody in this class." *Instead: "I'm not speaking to anybody in..."*
4. "I should have went to school yesterday." *Instead: "I should have gone to school..."*
5. "Me and Jim are working on..." *Instead: "Jim and I are..."*
6. "I didn't meet nobody." *Instead: "I didn't meet anybody..."*
7. "You saw who?" Instead: *"You saw whom?"*
8. "He followed Joe and I." Instead: *"He followed Joe and me."*
9. Answering a phone, "This is him," or "This is her." *Instead: "This is he," or "this is she."*

It's been argued that since those hearing these mistakes understand the meaning, "being particular about these distinctions is purely pedantic and arguably pretentious." That may be true, but incorrect usage still reflects on your intellect and may affect how you are perceived. That impression can make a difference in job placement, promotion, or other opportunities.

I still get together occasionally with one of my best friends from high school. We'll get together for lunch and talk about old friends or new experiences. Invariably, at several points in the conversation he will start using foul language.

I'm not sure why he uses salty language; he wasn't foul mouthed in school. I can tell you that it has affected where I'm willing to meet him for a meal and who else I might invite, since his behavior reflects on me.

These language skills must be used at all times, because you never know when someone will hear you and that might affect your next job or promotion.

### 2.18.7. *What to Talk About*

Two adages my mother taught me many years ago stand true today:

- Never talk about sex, politics, or religion.
- If you can't say something nice, don't say anything at all.

These two simple rules will eliminate arguments, bad feelings, and negative impressions.

### 2.18.8. *Cindy Had More to Say Than I Thought*

I was looking for a job while I was in college, and I applied to a radio station in downtown Wichita.

Cindy, the receptionist, seemed friendly enough. She took my name and asked me to wait a few minutes until Barry was ready to interview me. I returned for several interviews, and each time I spent about five minutes in the reception area before Barry's interview.

While the interviews with Barry went fine, what I didn't know until much later was that Barry asked Cindy for a report each time someone was interviewed. He wanted to know what the person did waiting for the interview, whether they could carry on a good conversation, if they used proper English, and how professionally they presented themselves.

Barry considered the opinion of Cindy nearly equal to his own. She could veto any hiring decision he made. Why? Because he figured job applicants were trying to look good for him, but they would relax and show their "real selves" to the receptionist.

You never know who will have input in these decisions.

And, yes, I got the job because I made good impressions on both Barry and Cindy.

### 2.18.9. *Make it a Habit; Do it Every Day*

I was at Disneyland once visiting with a Disney cast member at the Gallery in the old Bank on Main Street location. As we talked, I pointed across the square at City Hall to make a comment, and I pointed with two fingers.

He asked me if I had worked at Disney. "No. I do know it's part of *Disney* training, but I always point with two fingers because it's the *right thing* to do."

*Make it a habit.*

Is it easy to remember to point with two fingers? No, it's hard. So you have to practice constantly until you don't have to remember at all and it comes naturally. I learned to point with two fingers while walking around my neighborhood, pointing out homes, trees, dogs, and other sights to no one in particular.

That's true with eating habits, too, and with simple courtesies like holding the door for someone else.

In today's casual, fast-paced world we often find ourselves eating in front of the TV or at a fast food restaurant instead of a formal dining room table. Don't let this be an excuse for bad habits.

The only way you can get this right is to do it every day, every meal, every time you talk with family, friends, or coworkers, everywhere you go. It has to be natural, not something you have to think about.

For many jobs it seems unfair that these things could be a factor if your work is competent, and it's probably not part of the official job criteria. But people still react to your appearance and behavior.

It will help you get a job, keep a job, and get a promotion.

## 2.19. What to Do When You Get a Raise

Bank all the extra pay in your investment accounts every payday? That would be great for your investments, but maybe not so great for you.

Debt Builders typically celebrate first. Then they pay down a few bills. Finally they get in deeper. "After all," they reason, "making more means I can make more payments."

As a Wealth Builder you think the opposite, but celebrate a bit. You will have a plan that specifies a percentage of each paycheck that gets invested. You get the most and your investments get some. Stick with that.

## 2.20. Get Set Up for a Good Job While You're in College

Should you get a job while you're in college? Yes!

Should you go to work in a college office? Maybe. But only for awhile.

When Curtis was in college, he saw a sign taped to a door at school one morning that said American Express was interviewing seniors for fulltime IT jobs after graduation. He wasn't a senior, and he wanted part-time work right away. He went for an interview anyway, even though he was not a match.

They were impressed with him and hired him part-time. That worked out well and when he graduated they moved him to a fulltime position.

Grammy worked at the university in the office of one of the senior vice presidents. Part of her job was hiring and supervising student workers who were working to help pay their way through college.

That's *not* the kind of job you want, unless you want to work in a college office the rest of your career. (You *can* do that for a bit while you're looking for a more appropriate job.)

You need to determine where you want to work when you get out of college and try to land a part-time job *there*. If that doesn't work, look for a similar job at another firm doing the same thing.

Here's the reason.

If you do a great job, they like you and you like them. You're pre-trained and understand the company culture. When you graduate, they will probably hire you for a full-time position. If they can't, you're experienced and in a great position to take a similar job at another firm.

That's far better than heading to job fairs with no relevant job experience. Employers like to hire people who are experienced in their industry, and working as a college intern counts.

## 2.21.  What to Do If (When) You Lose Your Job

You *will* lose your job. *Or quit.* That's the nature of the business world today; you'll hold several jobs before you retire. Many things can cause this, including downsizing, job redefinition, or personality conflict. Or, you might not be just right for a job. The reason doesn't matter; what you do does matter.

It never seems to happen when it's convenient. It always comes at a bad time.

There have been several times when Grammy or I – or both of us – were without work. I was real proud of the fact that during those times I managed the finances so that we could maintain our lifestyle during the "off" time. Looking back, I see this was unwise and resulted in spending and creation of debt that was not in our best interest.

---

*Severance Pay and Unemployment Benefits, if you get them, are not vacation pay. These are temporary payments that give you a short amount of time to find a job and still have some money coming in. The goal is to have a new job well before these payments end.*

---

When you find yourself without an income, it's important to recognize that this is an instant transformation from an income to zero. That seems obvious, but it's so easy to try to maintain a lifestyle when you have severance pay, unemployment, or savings you can tap (we'll talk about a "Protection Fund" in a bit).

Yet these funds may have to last much longer than anticipated. It's the nature of being without a job that we don't know when paychecks will resume nor do we know how big they will be.

We all know people who have had times of unemployment that lasted about six months or more. Those were tough times, trying to make ends meet.

Curt told me, "We didn't have a paycheck for April and didn't get another one until the second half of December."

Did Curt have a Protection Fund in place? Yes. He shares, "We had about three months pay in the bank. It seemed like a lot at the time but not so much with the six more months without a check."

You may have some kind of offer or promise of a job but until it's a real job, giving you a real paycheck, don't count on it. I know too many people who have received this kind of promise and the promise did not come through.

It's easy to fool yourself into thinking a good job will "come along."

In the end, it's up to you to take care of yourself.

If unemployment runs out get a job – any job, full-time or part time – to get by while you continue to look for appropriate work. You really want to conserve funds during this period because you don't know how long it will take to find that job.

What can you do to preserve the money you have?

Cut expenses and adjust quickly. Don't wait until you've used up your savings or benefits before you cut spending.

During this time you need to know where every penny goes, so get a little notepad at the discount store and *log every expense*, even purchases of gum or coffee.

---

*No Income = No Spending. Go into "zero spending mode."*
*Think about the mindset you want when you're without income.*

---

Virtually all spending must stop when you're out of work. Now, I know you still have to eat, you still have rent, etc., but most expenses can be either reduced or stopped. The decisions on what to eat can be shifted to less expensive foods, eating at home instead of eating out, and using up those foods on the shelves in the kitchen that aren't your favorites but that you bought anyway.

You'll find a few tips in the chapter titled *Living the Wealth Builder Lifestyle*, but that's designed to help you with normal living.

Do you really need cable TV? Of course, you think you do, but could you live without it for a few weeks or even a few months while you go about the urgent hunt for a job?

More than once during these periods I recall thinking we needed a trip to Disneyland, and we made the trip, justifying it as a needed break or some such thing. Even though I was trying to do it "cheap" it probably cost me a thousand dollars or more. Each time. Big mistake.

It's time to *rethink all you spend*, starting from zero.

It may seem like a good time to paint the house or do repairs, in that you have the extra time. But you don't have the time (you're looking for work, remember?) and you may need the money for food or rent soon.

Of course, when you find that job and the paychecks start back up, you can reexplore the expenses you cut and establish a new Spending Plan.

# 3. Putting Money Away – The Plan

Jim Cramer of CNBC's *Mad Money* suggests that investing, not saving, is the key to financial security. Cramer was featured on CBS Sunday Morning (June 29, 2014) and said:

> *If you want to achieve real financial independence, then your paycheck is not going to be enough. And, contrary to what you might believe, saving isn't enough either. For true independence you need to invest your money so it grows year after year.*
>
> *First of all, there's two different kinds of investing, and that's why you should have two different portfolios.*
>
> *You've got your Retirement Portfolio ... pretty self-explanatory ... where you want to keep money in tax-favored vehicles like a 401-K plan or an Individual Retirement Account, IRA for short.*
>
> *...(and) Your Discretionary Portfolio is about creating wealth that you can actually use while you are still young enough to enjoy it!*
>
> *Retirement comes first, though.*
>
> *I recommend saving 10 to 15 percent of your income, with two-thirds of that for retirement investing. The rest you can play with in your Discretionary Fund.*
>
> *And if you don't have the time or inclination to pick individual stocks, by all means put your money in a low cost Standard & Poors Index fund.*
>
> *Bottom Line: Don't just save. Invest! And remember, always stay diversified, both in your tax-favored Retirement Portfolio and in your Discretionary account.*

My recommendation is a little more aggressive than Cramer's, because I want you to be a Wealth Builder, *more* than just financially secure.

And I think there are three things you need to put money away for:

- Retirement

- Wealth

- Protection

## 3.1. Retirement – 10%

I was a few years late when I started putting money aside for retirement. I had only about 30 years until I'd retire, but it's never too late, right?

I put two thousand a year into an IRA, about $166 a month. That was the limit for IRA contributions at the time. It was invested in a good mutual fund.

Grammy was also working so she did the same.

Making this investment was one of the smartest things I've ever done financially.

One of the stupidest things I ever did was that I stopped making the investment two years later. At least I was smart enough not to take the money out of the account.

It would have been better if I'd continued to make those investments, probably about two million dollars better.

The lesson here? Put 10% of every paycheck into investments for retirement.

---

*Set money from your wages aside for your retirement; 10% of your net check is recommended for retirement. And do it every month, every payday.*

---

### 3.1.1. IRA-Individual Retirement Account

The U.S. government in 1974 established tax-advantaged Individual Retirement Accounts which are offered by many banks and investment firms. These may give you the opportunity to invest and defer taxes on the earnings and growth in the account until you withdraw funds.

Unfortunately, not everyone can use an IRA. There are restrictions based on your income or employment status. And IRAs have limits on how much you can invest each year and penalties if you withdraw your money before the designated retirement age.

You can't take any money out of the IRA until you're nearly 60, and you are required to start taking money out in minimum amounts, currently starting at about age 70.

In general, place as much of your retirement investment as you can in an IRA because the investment can grow with taxes deferred until you take the money out, resulting in faster growth.

There are a couple of kinds of IRA, and the best choice for your investments is the *Roth IRA*. The money you put in will grow without taxes, and when you take it out after retirement you won't pay taxes either. It's one of the few real tax breaks that nearly everyone can enjoy. (You don't have to be wealthy to get this break... but I hope you will be by then!)

The IRS has a publication explaining what kind of IRAs are available, how much you can invest, and what tax opportunities might be. Fidelity, Vanguard, or another brokerage firm where you set up your IRA probably has publications that will help you as well, and they will handle the bookkeeping for you.

Your tax advisor (who helps you prepare your taxes) can help you decide how much you can put into an IRA. There are federal rules, and they change, so it's important to get tax advice that matches your situation.

My friend Marge heard that setting up an IRA was a good idea, so she set up an account with a brokerage firm. But it's been kept in *cash* all these years instead of being invested, so she has gained no advantages of tax-free growth. When you factor in inflation, she's been losing money all these years. It's like checking the balance at the end of each year and throwing five or six percent or so out on the street (the loss from inflation).

A lot of people set up IRAs with banks, too, who invest in long-term CDs at dismal rates, or in funds that the bank manages (adding to the bank's profits). You want to be more aggressive and get a higher rate of return at lower cost, so don't set your IRA up with a bank, use a low-fee brokerage firm like Fidelity or Vanguard.

One of the best things about an IRA is that *you* decide where your money is invested. Of course, that's good only if you have a sound investment plan (which you'll learn about in a few more pages).

### 3.1.2. *What about an Employer's Retirement Plan?*

If your employer offers a retirement plan, pension, 401-K, or SEP IRA, participate to the maximum available.

In addition to that, take 10% of your net check and invest it in a brokerage account which you dedicate to retirement.

Put as much of that in an IRA as you're allowed. (There are annual limits and restrictions if you have an employer plan.) Put the rest of the 10% in that brokerage account which you dedicate to retirement.

## 3.2.   Wealth – 10%

Retirement is only part of the picture.

As a *Wealth Builder*, you'll want to invest to build wealth, too.

I'm sharing a lot about retirement in this letter, but that's not the whole story. You want to build wealth, too. This is the piece of the formula that sets you ahead of those who are smart enough to build for retirement but not clever enough to have a wealth strategy.

This money should be allocated to a separate brokerage account for your wealth investments.

Then leave it there, growing, building wealth.

There's no magic about how you do this. Just deposit 10% of your check into the Retirement Account, and another 10% into the Wealth Account. But, wait! We're just getting started!

---

*Set money from your wages aside to build wealth; 10% of your net check is recommended for wealth building. And do it every month, every payday.*

---

## 3.3.   Protection – 10%

I once thought of this as a "Rainy Day" or "Emergency Fund," but I learned that the term Protection was better.

You could lose your job at any time. You want to build a war chest to cover job loss and unexpected expenses like major car repairs, home repairs, and medical expenses.

For this you want to have a three-year Protection Fund, enough to pay your bills and keep you going for three years with no income at all.

More than a quarter of Americans have no emergency savings, *USA Today* reported in June, 2014, quoting an annual survey by Bankrate.com. Of those who do have savings, 67% have less than six months worth of expenses. You want to do this better, by setting up a three-year protection fund and investing it so it grows much faster than a savings account.

This is money that you will need sometime and it not only protects you by providing funds, it also protects your retirement and wealth accounts by providing you additional assets.

---

*Set money from your wages aside for unexpected expenses; 10% of your net check is recommended for this. Do it every month, every payday.*

---

### 3.3.1. *Your 'Minimum Protection Balance'*

Determine the amount of cash you need on a monthly and annual basis and compute a three year amount. That's how much you want as a minimum in your Protection Fund.

One question: If you're adding 10%, won't that mean it will take 10 years to get one year's funds set aside, 30 years to get three? No. You're going to invest it, and, we hope, the invested money will deliver compound growth. If you get a 13% growth rate, it will take about 12 years to get three years' funds accumulated. Twelve years may seem like a long time, but it's far faster than 30 years! With fluctuating rates, your experience may be faster or slower. I'll explain about compound growth later, but, yes, it's amazing!

Until you have a full three years' cash put into your Protection Fund you may decide to pump more than the recommended 10 percent. In fact, this is a really good idea during those 12 years or so that it takes to reach your minimum so you already have excess funds you can use for those unexpected expenses. While those excess funds sit there they can be growing at a compound rate.

Since you want this in investments, too, and those values may vary, what do you do if the value falls below the three year amount? Add more funds.

Waiting to build a three year protection balance may seem daunting, so set interim goals like 3 months, 6 months, one year, and two years. You can have a little celebration as you reach each goal.

### 3.3.2. *Excess Protection Funds*

When the Protection Fund grows larger than your minimum you can use the excess for the rainy day or enjoyment purpose, which means funding a major car repair, dental bill, home repair, or, if the fund is large enough, a vacation.

When you have an emergency need, wouldn't it be great if you had enough excess funds in this account so you can just pay the bill and still have a three year cushion left in the account? That's the idea!

The three years amount is the minimum; the excess is where you pay out for emergencies.

What's your next car repair going to cost? No one knows. But recent repair bills for our cars have been over $3,000. Curtis told me recently about a repair estimate of nearly $6,000.

What about home repairs? Brian was quoted $8,000 for a new air conditioner.

In *The Millionaire Next Door*, it's revealed that the average decamillionaire has ten years worth of funds invested. That won't happen overnight, but it should be your ultimate goal.

There's no magic about how you do this, either. Just deposit 10% of your check into the Retirement Account, another 10% into the Wealth Account, and another 10% into your Protection Account.

You have to be a "future thinker" as you get this started. That means imagine what it will be like in a few years when you have built up your Protection Account and have a substantial cushion to protect you against job change and emergency repairs.

You'll have two accounts, the Retirement and Wealth accounts, that just grow and grow. And you'll have a Protection Account that grows but occasionally you will tap it to cover those financial emergencies, never letting it fall below your minimum protection balance.

### 3.3.3. *Saving Money*

Does all this have anything to do with saving money?

Sometimes people talk about "saving up" so they can buy a car, new furniture, or a tv.

That's a much better way to buy these things, much better than using credit, but it's not part of your Retirement Fund, your Wealth Fund, or even your Protection Fund.

### 3.3.4. *Lots of People are Living on 70% of What You Make*

"But Grandaddy," you ask, "why can't we enjoy our lives now? Must we wait until we retire?"

Sure, there's still 70%. Plan that well and you'll do fine.

In *The Richest Man in Babylon* (George S. Clason, 1926), Arkad asks the pertinent question:

> "How many of you have lean purses?" All of the men say that they have lean purses, that they have no money. "Yet," Arkad responds, "Thou do not all earn the same. Some earn much more than others. Some have much larger families to support. Yet, all purses are equally lean. Now I will tell you an unusual truth about men and the sons of men. It is this: That what each of us calls our necessary expenses will always grow to equal our incomes unless we protest to the contrary." Arkad tells the men not to confuse necessary expenses with their desires, that all men are burdened with more desires than they can gratify.

I don't care what you're making today, or next year, or ten years from now. There are lots of people getting by just fine on 70% of what you're making.

Many of them are living within those means. If they can, you can. *Live like that.*

Begin earning and investing early in your adult life.

It takes time to be a Wealth Builder. In *The Millionaire Next Door*, Stanley says Wealth Builders spend an about eight hours a month planning their investments. In just a bit, I'm going to show you a way to invest that lets you spend even less time, once you get going.

It doesn't take a lot of time but it does require that you pay attention, develop your financial plan and follow through so the wealth gets built.

## 3.4.   The 'Bad Magic' of Credit

Credit, especially using credit cards, is bad magic.

A few years back a friend (I'll call him Jeff) was approved for a credit card with a substantial credit line. He told me how surprised he was that he was approved, even more surprised at the credit line. He felt proud. He felt good.

Jeff was excited with his new credit card. "Let me buy our dinner tonight," he said, refusing my offer to pay for my own meal.

A year later Jeff had maxed-out the credit card and he had arranged payments with the bank's collection agency through payroll deductions to get it paid off. His interest bill was far larger than his purchases.

"Man, I wish I hadn't gotten that credit card," he told me.

Jeff was working to pay the bank, not to build his wealth or to pay living expenses.

When you are offered a credit card or store account, and when you are approved... *this is not a compliment. It's a business offer*. They are trying to sell you something. Yes, they think (hope) you will pay it off but if you stretch out payments or miss a payment they get big additional fees, and that's when they really profit.

### 3.4.1.   'Americans Have a Debt Problem'

"Americans have a debt problem," Jeanne Sahadi wrote for *CNNMoney* (July 29, 2014). "An estimated 1 in 3 adults with a credit history – or 77 million people – are so far behind on some of their debt payments that their account has been put 'in collections.' That's a key finding from a new Urban Institute study."

Putting overdue bills in collection means the creditor, a bank, a retail store, a service company, or other loan company, has given up on collecting the bill and given it to an outside collection agency. And it affects a borrower's credit rating.

That may not sound important but it can affect employers' hiring decisions, make it difficult to get a home mortgage or buy a car, and even increase insurance costs.

### 3.4.2.   Taking Debt to the Grave

More than 20% of young adults are overspending their income by a hundred bucks or more *every month*. It's a safe bet many of those are paying 25% or more on that as credit card debt.

Too many people rely on credit cards to make it to the next payday. This is disastrous. Some experts think the debt will grow and follow these people to their graves.

It's classic debt building.

And it's why it's important for you to think as a *Wealth Builder*.

## 3.5. What Banks Do and Why the Bank is Not Your Friend

We think of banks as places that have a lot of money. Here's what we're told:

*"Put your money in the bank for safekeeping."*

Because the government insures bank deposits, your deposits *are* safe. But that's only the beginning of the story.

First, think of the money you deposit in the bank as a loan to the bank. They pay you very little or nothing for it, but they have to give it back. They may not call it a loan, but it's just like a loan except the interest rate is virtually zero.

A bank president told me a few years ago he liked deposit accounts. "It's the cheapest money we can get!"

While your money is "in" the bank they loan your money to other people, even back to you, at a profit.

The bank loves it when you deposit money. And they love it when you borrow, because they can charge you so much in interest.

By the way, I'm not telling you that you shouldn't have money in the bank. You should. There are two points to this:

1. You shouldn't be borrowing a lot of money, either as a loan or through credit card debt.

2. You don't want to hold too much money in the bank; you want to invest it.

You already knew that, of course.

### 3.5.1. *Why Help the Bank Make a Lot of Money?*

Today's rates (probably different as you read this):

• Savings Account, 0.01% interest. Certificate of Deposit, 0.02% - 0.06%. (Chase, Bank of America, Wells Fargo).

• Prime Rate, 3.25%, reported in the Wall Street Journal.

• Auto Loan, 60 months, 3.17%.

• Home Mortgage, 15 years fixed rate, 3.27%.

• Credit Card Account, 16-25% Interest (sometimes more).

Think about that. If you loan the bank money (by putting money in a savings account) they pay you 0.1% interest. But if they loan you money (credit card) you pay them 25% interest... 250 times what they think it's fair to pay you! How is that fair?

That's how banks make money, by loaning out money at higher rates than they pay. These rates are too much. (Any rate is too much, really. It's just giving the bank money.)

The *Prime Rate* is the rate banks charge their best customers, and a few may even get below prime rates. Most of us pay considerably more, although auto and home loans are well secured and competitive enough that the rates are reasonable. But credit card rates are outlandish!

This chapter isn't about finding a good rate. It's to demonstrate how the banks make the money and we are the ones who pay.

Is it any wonder most Americans are broke?

Building wealth is about reversing that balance.

A few years ago Congress decided to do something about it. The law requires banks to print on credit card statements a notice revealing how paying the minimum amount will result in years of payments and outrageous amounts of interest paid. Most people don't read those; if they do, they ignore them.

Now you know why I talk about being debt free and paying off car loans and home loans fast.

### 3.5.2. Does the Banker Want to Help You? Or Just Sell You?

I think most bankers are in it for the money. Often, they get paid bonuses on how much they produce, which means how many loans they make.

Does that mean your banker will try to make you a loan even if it is not in your best interest? Probably.

There are exceptions.

I had dinner with a retired banker the other day who said his loan production went way down before 2008 when so many home loans were being made to people who really couldn't afford them. "I just couldn't justify making the loan. But it wasn't effective," he said.

"I knew that they just went down the street to someone else who did make the loan so they still ended up in trouble later trying to make payments."

Like getting a credit card offer, getting approved for a loan is not a compliment. It's just a banker trying to make money... *your money*.

### 3.5.3. Is There a Good Side to Credit?

"There are three types of 'good debt.'" says Manisha Thakor, author of *Get Financially Naked.* "First, mortgage debt, on a home that is reasonable relative to your income. Second, educational debt, on degrees whose prices are not higher than the income you expect to earn with the degree. And third, oddly enough, credit card debt that you pay off in full and on time at the end of each month."

Credit used wisely will give you a good credit score which will help you buy a home or a car.

A credit card may make it possible to rent a car, check into a nice hotel, or pay for an unexpected trip to the dentist.

You can also use credit cards to get cash rebates that you can plow back into your investment fund.

The key to credit cards, and most credit, is to pay it off, in full, on time, every month, so you never pay a dime of interest.

That means you have to keep track of your charges and be ready to make the payment. (Including that dentist's bill.)

---

*If you can't pay credit cards off each month,*
*cut them up and live without them.*

---

Still, if you're going to borrow, borrowing wisely is the key.

The mistake people make is using debt to close their budget deficit. When they don't have enough cash to pay for things they want or need, they make the purchases anyway, spending more than they make. The difference shows up in their climbing credit balances.

Even that unexpected dentist's bill should be covered by your Protection Fund. It may just take a few days to sell enough shares to get the cash to pay off the credit card.

## 3.6.  Investing in Yourself with Student Loans

A college education may give you just the skills and training you need to start a wonderful career.

But it could backfire.

At 23 years old Rosalyn Harris, an unemployed single mom, was convinced that getting a two-year degree in criminal justice  would position her for a new life. She signed up with Everest College in Chesapeake, Va., a for-profit college.

The school wooed her with job opportunities and student loans, reports Blake Ellis for *CNNMoney*. But, she says, classes were terrible, needed training was not provided, and she sought jobs for months after graduation without getting a call back.

Vantrell Echols, 36, from Georgia, signed up with for-profit Lincoln College of Technology back in 2008. What he got was a $20,000 debt and no job. Multiple employers told him his degree is not credible because other people they've hired from the school haven't had the necessary skills for the job. (*CNNMoney*, Nov. 2, 2014)

Even state universities and local community colleges have trouble placing students in jobs.

For-profit schools cost more and often deliver less, sometimes delivering nothing useful at all.

The answer? Choose a low-cost tax-supported state school or local community college, and investigate the program you plan to study beyond what the school's recruiters say.

And keep student loans to an absolute minimum. Graduating with $20,000 or more in loans is starting out with a problem.

Rosemary Anderson, 57, testified at a congressional hearing about taking out $65,000 in loans to pay for undergraduate and master's degrees. Then tough times came. She gave up on making payments. With interest and penalties the amount she owes has climbed by tens of thousands of dollars. "I will be indebted for life," Anderson testified.

Blake Ellis also reported for *CNNMoney* that more seniors are retiring still owing student loan debt. About 80% is debt financing their own education; 20% were loans taken out for a child or dependent. (*CNNMoney*, Sept. 10, 2014).

### 3.6.1. *Do You Actually Need a College Education?*

Your parents will be mad at me for saying this, but there are too many people graduating college today who are unable to find jobs in their field. It's important to think about your career path and the effect of a college degree.

If you're going to be a doctor, an accountant, a teacher, or an engineer, the degree is the ticket that lets you in. Certain careers require that ticket, and the career will define which degree you need.

For other career paths, maybe a two-year community college degree will be enough. Or maybe not. It's something to think about. If you're going to invest four to eight years and a ton of money, you want to be sure. It's more than just something to do.

A college degree *will* look good on your resume and may help you get a job or a better salary.

While in school and during summer breaks, get a job working in your intended industry. Get a bit of experience. It will give you an income, it will give you a head start, it will give you a taste of actually working in that field, and it might even give you a push to choose a different career path. If a change is possible, it's best to figure that out right away.

### 3.6.2. *Is It Wise to Get Student Loans?*

First, if you get a student loan it should be a government-backed student loan, not one through a private lender.

Second, your student loans should be relatively small. Schools and banks who handle student loans may be willing to let you roll all kinds of things into the bill covered by your student loan. This may let you run up a huge bill.

That's not a good idea.

There are many stories about people who owe over $100,000 when they get out of college. That's no way to start your career.

A better idea is getting a job and working your way through college.

Third, make all payments on time.

Tracy Bindel paid off her student loan 10 years early. It was a new year's resolution at a time when just sending the minimum payment was a struggle. Her older brother was her inspiration. "He always tells me that debt is an emergency like a flat tire or broken car," Bindel told Heather Long of *CNNMoney* (Dec. 3, 2014). "You would put all your money into those things really quickly without thinking about it."

She wrote her college loan balance on Post-It notes on her bedroom mirror and updated it with each payment. During the year she whittled that balance down from about $9,000 to $3,800 by mid-November. Cheap rent and frugal spending made the final push possible.

## 3.7.  The 'Other Side' of Credit – Compound Growth, *Real Magic!*

The idea of saving seems so dull, and it is!

"Saving money" is not much fun and will having you losing ground from the start.

But building wealth is exciting! And it is not the same as saving.

Invest intelligently and reinvest the earnings from your investments in order to build wealth and put yourself ahead of the savings and inflation rates.

### 3.7.1.  *The 'Positive Magic of Compound Growth'*

*Compound growth* occurs when you invest money and any income from that investment is rolled back into the investment so it, too, will grow.

---

*You don't take any earnings or growth from your investment.*
*You reinvest earnings so your investment grows faster and bigger.*

---

Here's a simple example, investing $1,000 and earning 13 per cent.

You invest $1,000. At the end of a year you've earned $130 (13% of the 1000). Instead of taking that money and spending it, you leave it invested.

Year 2: You have $1,130 invested. At the end of the year you've earned $147 (13% of the 1,130). Your total is $1,277. You leave it invested.

Year 3: You have $1,277 invested. At the end of the year you've earned $166. Your total is $1,443. You leave it invested.

Year 4: You have $1,443 invested. At the end of the year you've earned $187. Your total is $1,630. You leave it invested.

Year 5: You have $1,630 invested. At the end of the year you've earned $212. Your total is $1,842. You leave it invested.

Year 6: You have $1,842 invested. At the end of the year you've earned $239. Your total is $2,081.

In six years – without adding any funds – you have doubled your money.

To keep this example simple I've suggested that your earnings come at the end of the year, but investment value generally grows (or shrinks) constantly and dividends are paid quarterly. In other calculations in this letter I'll use monthly compounding (instead of annual compounding). That makes it a bit better; the $1,000 investment with monthly compounding would have grown to $2,172 in six years.

Here's a simple table that shows the growth on $1,000 over time.

Doubling in six years at 13% is pretty neat, but look what happens when you add a few more years:

### 3.7.2.  Investing $1,000 Once with Monthly Compounding at 13%

10 years: 3,643

20 years: 13,276

30 years: 48,377

40 years: 176,273

50 years: 642,292

60 years: 2,340,341

If you're 20 now that $1,000 will be worth $642,292 when you're 70. Wow! That's some difference!

### 3.7.3.  How Spending $1,000 Now Costs you $176,000

The chart shows that investing $1,000 today can be worth $176,273 in 40 years.

The other side of that is spending the $1,000 now means you can't invest it. And that means in 40 years you won't have the $176,000!

I find it helpful to think about spending money that way. That big screen TV that's on sale for just $899 (or about $1,000 with tax) may be a great deal, but it takes $176,000 out of my pocket later. Is that TV worth $176,000?

Maybe thinking about this will help you invest rather than spend.

By the way, part of the magic is investing at 13% or better. At 1%, the $1,000 would grow to only $1491 in 40 years. That's more like a savings account rate. There's no fun in that!

### 3.7.4.  *Monthly Investing is Even Better*

With monthly investing, you're adding money each month. If you invest $1,000 every month, in 12 months, that's $12,000. With 13% growth, compounded monthly, it will grow to $12879 by the end of the 12 months.

Again, you have the power of time on your side. Watch what happens when you invest $1,000 a month over a period of years:

$1,000 a month for 10 years: $246,680

$1,000 a month for 20 years: $1,145,519

$1,000 a month for 30 years: $4,420,646

$1,000 a month for 40 years: $16,354,337

$1,000 a month for 50 years: $59,837,525

$1,000 a month for 60 years: $218,278,661

This illustration is not very realistic because over the years your wages should increase and you can probably start investing more. The end amount can be staggering (as if the figures above aren't already staggering). Look at the next illustration.

### 3.7.5.  *Monthly Investing With Increasing Investments*

Over time, you should be earning more money and can invest more dollars in your investment program. Part of that will be inflation, and part a result of raises, promotions, and job changes.

For the next example we assume that you increase your monthly investment amount by three per cent each year.

For example, the first year you invest $1,000 a month. The second year you increase the monthly investment by three percent to $1,030 a month ($1,000 times 1.03). The third year you increase the monthly investment to $1,061 ($1,030 times 1.03). The fourth year you increase it to $1,093 ($1,061 times 1.03).

As you look at the monthly investment several decades down the road it may seem like a pretty big increase, but by then inflation will make it seem just as reasonable as $1,000 today. With increases in your earning power, you can *increase your investments even more*.

Again, you have the power of time on your side. Watch what happens when you invest an increasing amount over a period of years with a 13% return, compounded monthly:

10 years: $274,290 (Now you are investing $1,306/month)

20 years: $1,368,213 (Now you are investing $1,755/month)

30 years: $5,481,156 (Now you are investing $2,360/month)

40 years: $20,638,405 (Now you are investing $3,172/month)

50 years: \$76,096,601 (Now you are investing \$4,263/month)

60 years: \$278,479,781 (Now you are investing \$5,730/month)

By increasing your investment amount a mere three percent each year, you increase your 40-year results by over four million dollars!

## 3.8.   The 'Rule of 72'

You may hear someone talk about the "Rule of 72." The Rule of 72 states:

Divide 72 by the interest percentage per year to obtain the approximate number of years required to double your investment.

Remember when we computed the value of \$1,000 invested at a 13% growth rate? We more than doubled the amount in six years.

Applying the Rule of 72:

72 divided by 13 equals 5.53, or about five and a half years. (A financial calculator shows \$1,000 would grow to \$2,000 in 65 months or five years and five months. That's pretty close to the Rule of 72!)

Using the Rule of 72 assumes compound investing and, in practice, is not extremely accurate... especially with higher growth rates. The rule is useful for mental calculations and when only a basic calculator is available.

Sometimes you will find these referenced as the Rule of 70 or the Rule of 69. That's because under some circumstances those numbers are more accurate.

Financial calculators and spreadsheet programs have functions to find a more accurate doubling time.

## 3.9.   A Story About Compounding and Time

You're young, and it's easy to think you'll start "soon." Take note of the stories of Mary and Charlie.

---

*The numbers prove that the sooner you start, the better you'll do.*
*Invest and hold when you're young, then keep investing.*

---

Mary started investing \$1,000 a month when she was 20 and *stopped adding to her investment* when she turned 30 but she left the money invested, earning a 13% compound return on the *ten years* of \$1,000 contributions to her investment. When Mary turned 65 that investment had grown to \$22,779,644. Yes, that's over 22 and three-quarters of a million dollars.

Charlie invested nothing at 20, deciding to wait until he was a little older. When he turned 30, he started investing $1,000 a month, earning that same 13% compound return on the *35 years* of $1,000 contributions he made to his investment account. When Charlie turned 65, his account had grown to $8,523,183. That's over eight and one-half million dollars, Charlie did well, but not as well as Mary.

The point is this: The first ten years of investments are worth far more than the next 35 years of investments!

I wouldn't recommend stopping like Mary did, but starting early pays well!

What if you're already 30, or 40, or 50, or older? It's too late to gain the advantage held by a 20-year-old, but it's never too late to start. Starting now – today – is worth far more than starting later or not starting at all.

# 4. Investing: Growing Your Money Successfully

The only way to build real wealth is to own a business.

Owning a *small business*, however, is usually just buying a glorified job, and not such a great job at that! So you want to own a *big, successful* business like Walmart, General Electric, Coca-Cola, Disney, or Comcast. Owning a big business outright would take a lot more money than you and I have, so we settle by buying "part" of a big business, and we do that by buying *stock*, sometimes called *shares* because each share represents the share of the business you own.

---

*Yes, you can own part of a business and never have to create or sell a product, hire a staff, or attend a meeting. You just have to buy stock. It's better to own the company than to work for it or to loan it money. A few of us have come to realize that one of the main purposes of a job is to provide money to buy stock!*

---

Big businesses are owned by their *stockholders*, sometimes called *shareholders*, people who bought shares of stock in the business. You buy those shares by using the *stock market*, and you use an *investment firm*, *brokerage house*, or *stock broker*, to handle the purchase of those shares and, later, to sell them. This works so well that when you can afford it you can buy shares of many different businesses.

You make money two ways.

First, the *share price* of a share of stock in the company changes. If it goes up, the value of your investment goes up and you can sell the stock and get more cash than you spent buying it. That's how you make money. Of course, if the price goes down you could lose money.

When you sell for a higher price than you paid, the amount you gain (the difference between sale amount and purchase amount) is called a *profit* or a *capital gain.* If you sell for a lower price, the amount you lose (the difference between the purchase amount and the sale amount) is called a *loss*, a *capital loss*, or a *negative capital gain.*

Second, some companies pay stockholders *dividends*, sharing some of the profits with its owners. Generally, the companies that don't pay dividends are saving the cash to invest as they expand the company, or... they're not making money.

You want to invest in companies who will be successful and, as a result, their stock price will grow. The *risk* is that the stock price might fall. Also, some big, successful companies fail; their stock may have grown for years, but then their business changed and their investors lost money. An example would be Kodak, growing successfully through most of the last century, but failing as digital technology made film obsolete.

## 4.1.  The Stock Market is Legalized Gambling

The difference between gambling in Vegas or on the stock market is that in Vegas, everything favors the house. Over the long term, the house will win. On the stock market, over the long term the investor will win.

That assumes that the U.S. economy – and the world economy – will grow over time. History suggests that will be true, if for no other reason than the populations will grow requiring more and bigger business solutions to supply those populations.

It also assumes that the investor's strategy is sound.

> *In the 20th century, the United States endured two world wars and other traumatic and expensive military conflicts; the Depression; a dozen or so recessions and financial panics; oil shocks; a flu epidemic; and the resignation of a disgraced president. Yet the Dow rose from 66 to 11,497.*
>
> *– Warren Buffett*

Overall, we can expect the economy, and with it the stock market, to grow. The key for you is to invest intelligently so your "bets" are sound.

Some in the financial services world might argue that investing by owning shares in businesses is not gambling. I'm willing to concede that the risk goes down when you study your investment carefully, make intelligent decisions, and hold for the long term. The problem is that it's hard, if not impossible, to make those decisions.

Watch CNBC during market hours for a few days. The financial world has lots of advisors with opinions on which stocks to buy. But there are just as many advisors with opposite opinions. And those opinions change day after day.

In 2011, right after the 9-11 terrorist attacks, I decided to invest in airlines because I figured that prices of airline stocks would be down but people would still fly. I knew Southwest Airlines had made money every year since it went into business while other airlines struggled, so I bought stock in Southwest, figuring it was the best airline. Was this an intelligent decision?

Over the next ten years, Southwest continued to make money every year. The stock should go up, right?

During that time Southwest's stock fell from around $13 to below six dollars. This makes no sense to me, but the price changes on the whims of the market, not directly on the success of the business. The market's perception of Southwest was that it couldn't continue to make money, so the stock price went down.

(I'm happy to share with you that as I write this the stock price has recovered and is now over $34, not quite three times what I paid. And Southwest keeps making money.)

This is why I look at investing as gambling. You may come out ahead, or you may lose.

Did I make a sound buy with Southwest? It turned out okay. The point is that choosing individual stocks is a risky process.

Back in the 1980s I thought Ted Turner was a rebel broadcaster who just might make it big. Around the time he started CNN I invested in a few shares of Turner stock. (I knew this was a gamble.) It lost about half its value, then started back up. Eventually it merged with Time Warner and today it's worth 28 times what I paid.

Another smart buy? I like to think so, but "a lucky buy" is probably more descriptive.

I remember a day back in 1986 when Dad and I had a phone discussion about a new stock trading the next day on the stock market. The "talk" was that it would grow fast but I'd had a bad customer service experience with the company. Neither of us invested in it.

That was a smart move, even though hindsight tells us what we missed. Ten thousand dollars invested in Microsoft in mid-March, 1986, would be worth about 4.3 million dollars today! (Not that I could have invested that much.)

We had a similar talk about Google when it was listed on the stock market. I told Dad, "Search engines come, and search engines go," which was true at the time. Neither of us bought. Big mistake?

In fact, investing in any individual stock is risky.

Back in the early days of personal computing, an investment in Microsoft, Apple, or Intel would have resulted in handsome growth. But at the time there were hundreds of other companies in that industry, all claiming that *they* would be the amazing growth company. Choosing the right company? Nearly impossible.

When I moved to Phoenix in 1985 I discovered Flakey Jakes, a fun restaurant with good service and good food. I reasoned it would be a good investment. It was young, but one of the founders of Pizza Hut had just invested in it so I figured I had a winner. Flakey Jakes didn't just go down, it went out! The company folded and my investment was lost.

As the dot-com boom started in the late 90s I learned that Vitamin Shoppe was expanding and starting an online operation. You could buy stock in their new online company, VitaminShoppe.com. I was already a Vitamin Shoppe customer, so I figured the online business would be good (and I'm sure it is today). But their online business hemorrhaged money, paying and overpaying, I think, for software to run the online store. Before it could begin to turn a profit, they closed it down and it was bought back by the main company. For me, another loss.

Picking winning stocks is hard. It's easy to choose a loser.

## 4.2.  My Friend Gambles in the Stock Market

"I use Fidelity for my investments," Don told me. He was doing some work in my home and spotted a Fidelity envelope in the mail I had just retrieved from the mailbox. "I really like their online capability because I can buy or sell stocks quickly for just eight bucks a trade."

"Really," I responded. "You trade very much?"

"Sometimes more than I should," he said. A couple of months ago I totaled up the commissions I had paid that month and it was $2,800."

"Hmmm," I reacted. "I prefer to buy a good mutual fund and hold it."

That was the end of our discussion, but let me tell you something about Don that he doesn't know.

He doesn't *invest* in the stock market. He *gambles*.

That $2,800 in commissions? Those are trading fees, not investments. At eight dollars each, that's about 350 trades... in one month! He's buying and selling a lot, and at the end of the month he's probably sold nearly everything he bought.

There's a term in the business for Don. It's *trader*. I think Don may hold a stock for a few days or even weeks, but he's in and out, gambling that the stock will go up before he needs the money. He may have kept a few stocks longer than a day, but that's not his game. He gets a thrill out of buying and selling. In my book, that's gambling.

It's not what you want to do.

In the short term, stocks rise and fall based on the whims of the market.

## 4.3.  How Hard Is It to Invest in the Market?

*"When we own portions of outstanding businesses with outstanding manage-ments, our favorite holding period is forever."*

*– Warren Buffett*

Warren Buffett and his staff spend a lot of time investigating the companies where they choose to invest. Warren Buffett is a great investor.

Do you have to be a great investor to make money in the stock market?

No.

But you have to be smart.

*"You don't need to be an expert in order to achieve satisfactory investment re-turns. But if you aren't, you must recognize your limitations and follow a course certain to work reasonably well. Keep things simple and don't swing for the fences. When promised quick profits, respond with a quick 'no.'"*

*– Warren Buffett*

The smart move is to diversify your investments and don't try to pick individual stocks.

---

*Buy a no-load mutual fund. (But not just any no-load mutual fund.)*

---

"A mutual fund pools money together from thousands of small investors and then its man-ager buys stocks, bonds or other securities with it," *Money* magazine senior editor Walter Updegrave explains.

"You get a stake in all its investments."

"That's a big deal: Since most funds allow you to begin investing with as little as a couple thousand dollars, you can attain a diversified portfolio for much less than you could buying in-dividual stocks and bonds. Plus, you don't have to worry about keeping track of dozens of hold-ings – that's the fund manager's job." (*CNNMoney* online, *Mutual Funds Explained*)

Generally, when I talk about a *fund*, I'm referring to a stock fund, that is, a mutual fund that invests primarily in stocks as opposed to one that invests in bonds or other securities.

### 4.3.1.  A Mutual Fund Illustration

Let's explore the S&P 500 Index, a well established list of the 500 biggest businesses in the United States.

If you wanted to invest directly in those 500 companies, you'd have to buy at least one share of each. At an average price of, say $75, you'd be paying $37,500. Plus, you'd have brokerage fees of $4,000 or more and a lot of work just getting it all ordered. Total: $41,500.

Every time you wanted to invest a bit more, you'd need to have $41,500 and be ready to place 500 orders again.

You'd also need to watch the S&P Index news for any companies that are changed in the list. A change would require you to sell the stocks of the companies who are removed and to buy replacement stocks in the companies that are added.

That's a lot of money, and a lot of time, and a lot of work.

And, really, it's not that simple. Because the price of a share of stock in one company isn't equivalent to the share of another company, you should be buying more of some firms and less of others. This adjustment, called *weighting*, is computed by the S&P folks, and it would be a hassle to represent it in your investments. To do it properly, you'd need to be buying a lot more than one share of each at a time, probably investing $500,000 a pop.

Ready for all that?

I thought not. There is an easier way.

Invest at least $2,500 in a mutual fund that tracks the S&P 500 Index. The managers who run the fund do all that work on a big scale, and you own just a tiny bit of the pie. But for $2,500 you can get your start. Yes, you own, indirectly, a part of all 500 companies. And you can add in any amount, even $50, and still be getting a little bit more ownership of all 500.

They do charge you a small percentage of your investment as a fee for all that. This is called a fund's *expenses*. On a $2,500 investment the fee works out to about $2.50 a year. Wow! I think it's worth it!

Over time, the value of your investment should grow and you'll invest more money, so the expenses percentage will work out to more money, too. That's how the fund makes money.

> *"There are only two guarantees in the financial business. If you buy an index fund you'll get the market return, and if you don't invest at all you'll get nothing."*
>
> – John Bogle, Vanguard founder

## 4.4. Pick the Right Mutual Fund

Like picking stocks, it's important to pick the right mutual fund. You want to choose a fund with the right managers and with low expenses and no load or commissions. (I'll explain that in a moment.)

The fund managers decide which stocks to buy and when to get out of a stock and move to a different company.

When you buy a mutual fund, you may be asked if you want to reinvest distributions. Yes, you do, because you want it to grow as much as possible.

Remember how I lamented not buying Microsoft or Google? Well... because I invested in certain mutual funds, and *those funds invested* in Microsoft and Google (and Apple, Facebook, Berkshire-Hathaway, Exxon-Mobil, Johnson & Johnson, Wells Fargo, Chevron, Proctor & Gamble, etc.), I was indirectly invested in those companies and didn't know it. *I could have paid more attention* to the reports from the funds and I would have known. I let them do their job, and they did it well. I didn't actually *need* to know!

I'm pretty sure none of these funds invested in Flakey Jakes or the VitaminShoppe.com online venture. Point made?

---

*It's hard to choose winning stocks. It's much easier to choose winning mutual funds... if you pay attention to the methods I'm revealing here.*

---

## 4.5.  Do You Pay Extra to Invest in a Mutual Fund?

Yes, but you'll pay brokerage fees if you invest directly in stocks without using a fund. So you pay something either way. With a well-managed fund your investment is managed daily and diversified over more stocks than a small investment could be.

The average actively managed stock fund charges 1.26% of assets a year for *expenses*. That comes directly from your returns, so *you want funds with expenses well below that average.*

The two largest fund companies are Fidelity and Vanguard. Both tend to charge lower than average fees. Dad liked Fidelity. Mom liked Vanguard, probably just to be different. They're both excellent firms.

I got started with Fidelity and it was a good experience. As I was putting this letter together I looked up some of the fees they charge. (These may be different by the time you read this.)

### 4.5.1.  *Passively Managed and Actively Managed Funds*

***A passively managed fund, also known as an "index fund,"*** is one which follows a standard industry index like the S&P 500 Index. All the managers have to do is balance the holdings in the fund to approximate the blend of stocks in the index. That's relatively easy, so the fees should be substantially lower.

The Fidelity S&P 500 Tracking fund, which they call the *Fidelity Spartan 500 Index Fund*, charges 0.095%. That's less than one-tenth of a percent. When you convert those funds to their Spartan 500 *Advantage* Class (after your investment has grown to cover the $10,000 minimum investment), it falls nearly in half to 0.05%.

That works out to about $50 for a $100,000 investment in the fund.

**An actively managed fund** is one where the managers analyze companies and the managers decide where and how much to invest in each one. This takes a lot of research and expert decisions, and that costs the fund more, so the expenses are higher.

Expenses on some of the actively managed funds I hold are:

- Fidelity Select Health Care Portfolio, 0.77%

- Fidelity Select Biotechnology Portfolio, 0.76%

- Fidelity Select Multimedia 0.81%

That means the expenses for these funds are about $800 on a $100,000 investment, 16 times more than an index fund. When you pay this much more you expect more growth. Sometimes you get it and sometimes you don't, so selecting an actively managed fund requires some attention.

These three actively managed funds invest in special sectors of the overall market, rather than following a published index. Their managers have to invest time and resources into evaluating stocks, so the expenses are higher, but still about 35% less than the average actively managed stock fund.

As you get to the *plans* you'll see I suggest a mix of passively and actively managed funds.

### 4.5.2. What's a 'Load?'

You have to pay a *load* fee when you buy mutual funds from a broker, financial planner, insurance agent or other adviser and sometimes when you buy from the fund manager. There are load and no-load funds.

There are plenty of no-load mutual funds. So *never* pay a load.

By the way, most funds have a redemption fee if you sell a mutual fund investment that you've owned only 30-90 days. That shouldn't ever be a problem since you will buy to keep a long time.

### 4.5.3. Tax Consequences with Mutual Funds

Owning mutual funds does have some tax consequences each year that can affect your total tax bill.

If you own stocks, some of them pay dividends which are taxable. If you sell stocks, any gain is taxable as what is called *capital gains*.

When you own a fund, the fund receives dividends and is always buying and selling stocks. A portion of that is yours, which you should have automatically reinvested. Still, it's taxable, and you'll receive a tax statement each year that will need to be part of your income tax preparation.

Taxes on capital gains and dividends on stocks held for a long term are generally lower than taxes on wages.

## 4.6. Continuous Automatic Investing

Sometimes mistakenly called "Dollar Cost Averaging," *Continuous Automatic Investing* means you make a monthly investment of a specified dollar amount with no regard to the current market conditions. By investing regularly, you have the advantage of investing as soon as the money is available, and you "average" the cost of buying your investments without worrying whether your purchase is at a stock market *high* or *low*.

This removes the stress of trying to time the markets, something even experts are unable to do consistently.

Each payday, you make the regular investments into your portfolios, confident that over the *long term* market prices will rise more than they fall.

## 4.7. What Are Bonds?

You often hear about "stocks and bonds." Should you be buying bonds?

As people get older many want to start to invest a portion of their total investment in bonds. Bonds usually don't fluctuate in value as much as stocks, so the idea is they are unlikely to lose much value even when the stock market moves down. (Of course, they won't rise when the stock market goes up, either.)

A bond is really a loan. It's you loaning a government or a corporation some money for a particular period of time. They pay interest for that, and that's how you make money. When the bond comes due, they pay you back, with interest.

There are a couple of catches.

First, if you want to cash out early you generally have to find someone to buy the bond from you. A brokerage house may be able to do that for you, but they charge a fee for that. If the going interest rates have changed upward the value of your bond will have gone down, maybe below what you paid for it. (Likewise, if rates have gone down, your bond may have increased in value.)

Second, you can buy bond funds, which is like a stock mutual fund but they invest in bonds. When interest rates go down the value of the fund goes up, and when rates go up the value of the fund goes down. I think it's less an investment and more like gambling on interest rates. Don't invest in bond funds.

If you're inclined to invest money in bonds, a smarter move would be to buy bank CDs or "treasuries," obligations of the federal government. Don't try to cash them in early.

Look for a good rate, which may be hard to find. Even the best rates will probably return less than inflation, so it's a losing proposition. The strength is that in times when the stock market goes down, your CDs and treasuries will not lose value.

## 4.8.  Other Market Products You Might Consider

The financial markets have lots of different products where you can invest, including ETFs, options, derivatives, commodities, penny stocks, etc.

My advice: *Don't*. Just stick with mutual funds that invest in stocks. It's easier and safer.

You may hear about ETFs which are *Exchange Traded Funds*, and are very similar to mutual funds. There are some short-term tax advantages with ETFs, but it is harder to manage reinvestments and your monthly investment allocations. Since you want this to be easy, stick with the mutual funds.

## 4.9.  Two Strategies for Investing

I'm going to share two strategies for choosing where to invest. One is very easy. The other takes a bit of time, study, and risk.

Neither plan requires you to read *The Wall Street Journal*, follow stocks on CNBC, or subscribe to any of the expensive investment advisory services.

## 4.10.  Strategy A – The Easy Way

The easiest investment strategy involves a broad and balanced investment in the 500 best U.S. stocks.

The easy way to do that is using a low expense index tracking mutual fund that tracks the S&P 500 Index. That's because the index is well diversified. It doesn't focus on any one sector; the index is based on the leading 500 companies in the United States as determined by Standard & Poor's.

---

*With an index fund you're automatically diversified and investing in U.S. business across the board. And it's easy because you buy one thing and the mutual fund manager balances all the stock investments.*

---

This is pretty close to Warren Buffett's plan for his heirs after he dies, as reflected in the instructions to his trust managers (See the appendix at the end of this letter.)

Will your investment grow? Yes, and no. Over the last 25 years or so the annualized return has been about 9.5% per year. Since that includes the "Dot-Com Crash" and the "Great Recession," that's pretty good.

There *are* years when it goes down (including 2008, the main year of the recession).

The market is loosely defined as the S&P 500, so if you're invested in an S&P 500 Index tracking fund, you're matching the market. Really, Strategy A is just a way to match the market, using a low-expense mutual fund to do it.

It probably will not match the 13 percent that I used in my illustrations of compound growth, however. If you want to do that, you'll have to "beat" the market.

Does the difference between 9.5% and 13% make much difference? That's a decision you have to make. Remember how putting in $1,000 now can grow to $176,000 in 40 years at 13%? That same $1,000 will grow to about $44,000 in 40 years at 9.5%, making the difference between 9.5% and 13% worth $132,000. Wow!

That's why I like Strategy B best. But if you don't want the hassle, or if you find it hard to understand Strategy B, or if you'd rather minimize risk, go with Strategy A. There's nothing wrong with that.

There's not much more to say about Strategy A because it's just this simple: Put your investment money into a low-expense S&P 500 Index tracking fund. If you really want the easy way, this is it.

## 4.11.  Strategy B – Just a Bit Harder

Strategy B is a little more complex and requires some time, some analysis, and some risk.

In return you have an opportunity to "beat the market" and reach the 13 percent I used in my illustrations. Maybe you'll do even better.

Of course, you could do worse, so be forewarned that when I say there is risk there really is. We minimize that risk with a couple of very simple allocations.

Your *portfolio* is your investments. If you follow Strategy A, it's very simple. You put everything into your S&P 500 Index tracking fund so *that's* your portfolio.

Strategy B complicates that by having you allocate money each month into several different funds. This is pretty easy to do, but you'll end up with a portfolio consisting of several different funds.

## 4.12.  Mutual Funds Are Not All Created Equal

I'm going to share with you my methods for choosing mutual funds and my strategy for diversification.

We've already mentioned the index funds. There are a number of index funds, but the only one I'm suggesting is a fund that tracks the S&P 500 Index. That's what Warren Buffett suggests, and if it's good enough for him it's good enough for me.

> *Always be diversified. This sounds simple, but it takes discipline.*
>
> *In short, you are diversified when no more than 20 percent of your portfolio is in the same sector, the same area of the economy.*
>
> *That way if something happens to crush one group of stocks, like the tech crash of 2000 or the financial crisis starting in 2008, it won't eviscerate your entire portfolio.*
>
> *– Jim Cramer, CNBC's Mad Money*

## 4.13. Sector Investing

One way to do even better is to invest part of your money in certain sectors of the business world that you think will grow more than the rest. If you choose the sector properly, it can be quite rewarding. But, as Cramer advises, avoid some risk by limiting your exposure in any one sector to 20% of your total investment.

My first mutual fund, where I stared investing in 1983, was Fidelity Magellan. For years it was one of the top growth mutual funds, investing in a diversified selection of stocks. Magellan was managed by Peter Lynch who has now reached legendary status in mutual fund circles because he was so good at what he did.

Magellan, in its time, was a great fund. I did well with it. (After Lynch retired, Magellan didn't do so well.)

But Magellan is not the kind of fund you want to buy even though it's still offered. Why?

Because it's not a fund that's focused on a sector. It's more like an index fund, only with higher expenses. During Lynch's management, it did very well. But in later years it bounced above and below the S&P 500 as often happens with these funds that try to beat the index.

That's why the Plan B financial strategy includes a low-expense S&P 500 Index tracking fund, plus three actively managed *sector* funds of your choice. At Fidelity's website, I specify *Sector Equity* in my search. Stocks are grouped into different sectors depending upon the company's business, not on its size, location, or dividends. This gives me actual business sectors like health, technology, industrials, financial, consumer cyclical, utilities, and real estate.

Avoid choosing based on stock market categories like Large Growth, Large-Cap, Small-Cap, Mid-cap Value, Large Blend, or Emerging Markets. These are stock market terms for the size of a company or its apparent emphasis on dividends or growth.

### 4.13.1.  *You Want to Pick Winning Sectors, Not Stocks*

You pick sector funds based on *industries you think have good growth potential*, combined with an examination of the numbers for the available sector funds, showing relatively good returns for 1-year, 3-years, 5-years, and 10-years.

---

*The secret to beating the S&P 500 is picking industry sectors that you think will beat the index and then choosing appropriate funds within the sectors.*

---

In case you pick wrong, with Strategy B you protect yourself by investing in more than one sector and you also maintain a healthy investment in a S&P 500 index fund.

### 4.13.2.  *A Real Life Comparison of Four Funds*

Let's compare several real mutual funds and look at their hypothetical gains and losses over ten years. As I write this in 2014, it's a particularly good time to look at historical returns because there has been growth, followed by the devastating "Great Recession" which started in 2008, followed by growth. A 10-year view of gains and losses tells a lot.

**Fidelity Spartan 500 Index Fund - Advantage Class** is broadly diversified through the U.S. economy, investing in common stocks included in the S&P 500 Index.

$10,000 invested on August 31, 2004, for ten years would have grown to $22,285 by 2014. That's more than double the original investment, including a major drop during the financial crisis of 2008.

During that financial crisis the fund dropped, reducing the value to $7,284 on Feb. 28, 2009, but that recovered to $22,285 by Aug. 31, 2014.

**Fidelity Select Multimedia Portfolio** is a managed fund focused on companies engaged in the development, production, sale and distribution of goods or services used in the broadcast and media industries.

$10,000 invested on August 31, 2004, for ten years would have grown to $31,603 by 2014. That's more than *triple* the original investment, including a major drop during the financial crisis of 2008.

During that financial crisis the fund dropped, reducing the value to $6,495 on Feb. 28, 2009, but that recovered to $31,603 by Aug. 31, 2014.

I like this illustration because it shows that this managed sector fund was lower than the index fund at its lowest, but its recovery was also stronger resulting in an outstanding return.

**Fidelity Health Care Portfolio** is a managed fund focused on companies engaged in the design, manufacture, or sale of products or services used for or in connection with health care or medicine.

$10,000 invested on August 31, 2004, for ten years would have grown to $38,860 by 2014. That's *almost four times* the original investment, including a major drop during the financial crisis of 2008.

During that financial crisis the fund dropped, reducing the value to $9,115 on Feb. 28, 2009, and that recovered to $38,860 by Aug. 31, 2014.

I like this illustration because it demonstrates that some sectors fare better than others, and that's why we diversify.

But look at banking.

**Fidelity Select Banking Portfolio** is a managed fund focused on companies engaged in banking.

$10,000 invested on August 31, 2004, for ten years would have grown to only $11,629 by 2014. That's a *disappointing return.* The 10-year average annual return is only 1.52%, including a major drop during the financial crisis of 2008.

During that financial crisis the fund dropped, reducing the value *way down* to $3,687 on Feb. 28, 2009, and that recovered to $11,629 by Aug. 31, 2014.

I like this illustration because it demonstrates that some sectors fare worse than others, and that's why we diversify. You might have thought banks would be a secure investment, but financial stocks were particularly hard hit in 2008-2009.

I'm happy I was not invested in the Select Banking Portfolio, *but...*

Instead *I was invested in just one bank stock*, Bank of America. To compare, a $10,000 investment in Bank of America August 31, 2004, dropped *way down* to just $888 by Feb. 28, 2009, and grew back to only $3,620 by August 31, 2014. Pretty sad. It shows the danger of investing in one stock; the mutual fund was dismal, but *much* better than that one stock. Those mutual fund managers still invested in bank stocks, but they chose better than I.

As Jim Cramer advised, diversify your investments, putting no more than 20% into any one sector.

Add my advice: Invest in a good mutual fund and stick with it.

---

*It's hard to choose winning stocks. It's much easier to choose winning mutual funds if you follow the methods I'm sharing in this letter.*

---

## 4.14. How to Choose an Actively Managed Mutual Fund

Online tools from Fidelity make comparing mutual funds pretty easy. (Vanguard has a similar tool but offers very few sector funds, making it difficult to use Vanguard for Strategy B.)

I use Fidelity's Mutual Funds Research tool on their website that brings up a list of funds. You can specify what you're looking for like I do:

- Asset Class: Sector Equity.
- Fidelity Funds Only. You want no fees to purchase.
- No Transaction Fee Funds Only. Some funds charge a load or transaction fee when you buy, others when you sell. Again, you want no extra fees.
- Morningstar Rating: 4 Stars (Includes 5 stars). Morningstar is a firm that evaluates stocks and investments. Their top ratings are 4 and 5 stars; I want to reduce my risk so I choose from the funds they think are best.

Then I look at the 1-year, 3-year, 5-year and 10-year returns. While there's no certainty that past results will continue in the future, it's the only handle we have on growth. You want a fund with consistent growth.

Funds with the biggest growth numbers may also carry the biggest risk. That's why you want to look at *all* the numbers, one-year, three-years, five-years, and ten-years, and compare them fund to fund.

From this I get a good idea of what funds are available.

Don't just pick the top funds. Pick sectors that make sense to you, and click through to look at the fund itself. Check:

- Fund Overview. This describes what the goals of the fund are.
- Expense Ratio (Net). Again, you want low expenses.
- Minimum to Invest. Make sure this is a fund you can afford to buy. (I've seen funds with a minimum of five million dollars, intended for big institutional investors. There's no reason to waste any time looking at one of those.
- Top 10 Holdings. These are the top ten stocks the fund has bought. These need to make sense to you. If you want, you can look up information on each of these stocks to learn more. Keep in mind that the manager may change the stock mix at any time in order to try to keep the fund growing.

Find three funds you like in *different* sectors.

A health care fund and a pharmaceuticals fund would both be in the health sector, so if you determine you want to invest in health you'd choose only one of these funds, not both.

I remember once looking for a real estate fund, one that invests in real estate properties and builders. I thought real estate must be a profitable investment, and investing through a fund would be much smarter than buying properties. But as I searched through the funds list, the numbers just weren't there. I chose something else.

I like to make the final decision based on what stocks the fund is holding. Do these look like businesses that make sense to me?

## 4.14.1. *What Sectors Should You Choose?*

Sector choice is up to you, of course, but I suggest making it something you have some interest in and something you believe has a long-term future. These sector funds should also look good in the numbers as you do your research.

I'll share my current sector choices, but not as a recommendation. You should *do your own study* to determine what's right for you. I'm currently investing in:

- Health Care. This seems like a growing industry. Hospitals are getting bigger, drugs are costing more, and doctors continue to refer to other doctors. The folks in our family go to the doctor a lot!

- Multimedia. I like companies like Disney who create entertainment and the cable companies who deliver content. It seems as if Americans keep seeking entertainment, and we are no exception.

- Software and Computer. Partly because I work in information technology, I think there's a big future here.

Could any of these sectors of the economy possibly get less important? I think not. (But I know I could be wrong, or that the investment values could go down. Still, I look at the numbers to make the decision.)

This is the kind of thinking that I use to decide where to invest. The sectors make sense to me, and when I look at the numbers it holds up. These funds are all near the top of the list, but don't seem too risky.

Look at the available funds. *What makes sense to you?*

---

*Think about the future and choose your sectors carefully. Investing in a sector fund involves more risk than investing in the index fund. That means more opportunity for growth and more risk for loss. Choose industries you think have the greatest likelihood of growth over the coming decades.*

---

## 4.15. How to Diversify Your General and Sector Investments

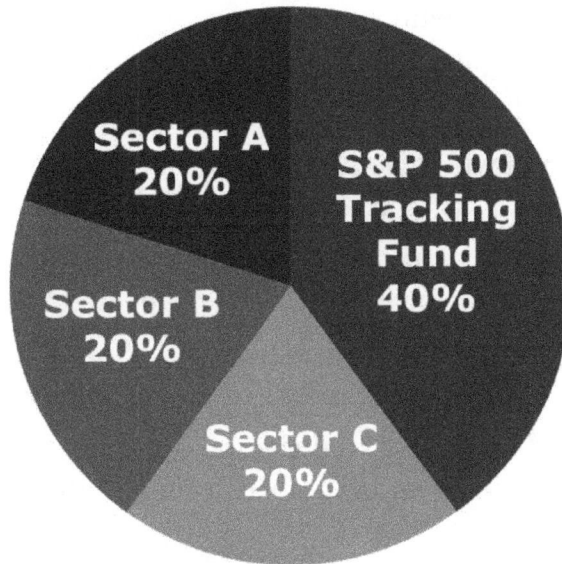

For Strategy B, I suggest you invest in the following proportions:

- 40% in the S&P 500 Index tracking fund.

- 20% each in three different sector funds of your choice. I don't know what you'll choose, so I'll call them Sector A, Sector B, and Sector C.

For example, if you are investing $1,000 each month you'd invest:

- $400 in the S&P 500 tracking fund.

- $200 in the Sector A fund.

- $200 in the Sector B fund.

- $200 in the Sector C fund.

These may be distributed among your various accounts as necessary to maintain appropriate balances.

Is this hard to do? No, just deposit one check in your account by mail, or transfer the money from your bank with a phone call or using your smartphone. Wait for it to clear, then call and give instructions on how to invest it, or do it online.

The result is easy to manage, yet gives you the opportunity for extra growth by choosing higher-growth sectors for part of your investment.

## 4.16. What to Do When the Market Goes Down

Will the market go down? Yes, it will!

As I write this "The Fed" has set interest rates very low, near zero. This is the rate banks pay to get money from The Fed, and rates banks charge corporate America are low, too.

The "big fear" is that The Fed will raise rates and send the stock market into a tailspin.

And the truth is that The Fed probably will raise rates soon, a bit at a time, and with each raise the stock market will decline temporarily. That's a normal thing. No matter what the current rate, The Fed will raise rates, or lower rates, and it will affect the market temporarily.

And that's only one thing that will affect the market. Sometimes it's war, economic news, politics, problems in certain big companies or industries, or even just the weather.

If you watch the news, you'll discover that the market is up because of a certain thing happening, and another time the market is down because of the same thing happening. Frankly, there's little logic.

Remember what I said about gambling? Remember I said the difference with this kind of gambling is that *over the long term*, if you're invested right, you win? (That's not how it works in Vegas.)

When the market goes down what should you do? Nothing. Keep on investing.

*Motley Fool's* Todd Campbell says he's really glad he kept investing monthly during the financial crisis of 2008. His biggest regret? "I didn't significantly boost my monthly contributions. If I had, then I would have seen a much bigger increase in my portfolio value when the S&P 500 eventually stopped falling and then doubled." (*CNNMoney,* "My Biggest Investing Regret," May 28, 2015)

Most people panic and sell when the market goes down. (And they get excited and invest when the market is high.) That's not what you want to do!

A friend of mine told me that when the market dives, she tells her friends, "If you sell now, you've already lost 20%. By the time the market's gone back up enough that you decide to buy it will be back up 30%. Right there you've lost 50%. Just stay invested and ride it out."

What if there's a month when everything goes down? Or a bad year? It happens!

Since I've been investing I've seen ups and downs and some of the downs have been doozeys. I suffered the Crash of 1987, the housing crash of 1990, the dot-com crash of 2000-2001, and the banking-mortgage crash of 2008. My holdings went down. A lot. Especially in that last one.

No experts actually know when the market will go up, and when it will go down. Yes, there are experts with opinions, but this week's star expert won't hold that position long.

## 4.17. What's a 'Stock Market Correction?'

A stock market correction is when the stock market declines 10% or more in a short period of time.

"It's a natural part of the stock market cycle," writes Kimberly Amadeo, U.S. Economy Expert, writing for *About.com* (Sept. 5, 2014) .

"A stock market correction can be caused by some kind of event that creates fear and subsequent panicked selling... However, that's exactly the wrong thing to do. Why? The stock market usually makes up the losses in three months or so. If you sell during the correction, you will probably not buy in time to make up your losses."

Corrections will occur, and you'll worry. When that happens, remember that I warned you, and relax. With your financial plan, things should self-correct in time.

## 4.18. What About Major Crashes?

A crash is bigger, but the net effect is the same. People get excited and sell, and as more people sell prices go further down, causing more excitement and more selling.

If the market is crashing... or one of your mutual funds seems to be crashing... should you ignore it?

No. But it's not time to panic, to let fear guide your decision, or to let a "gut feeling" scare you out of the market.

You can reevaluate your investments.

What if you lose half of your investment? We never like to see a market crash and significantly hurt your total investment. But it does happen. I'm sorry. I feel for you. But stay the course.

In the chapter on where and how to invest, I gave you a "real life comparison" of several mutual funds. I told you about what happened over a ten year period, which happened to include the financial crisis of 2008. That crisis is often called the "Great Recession." It is also referred to as the "Lesser Depression," the "Long Recession," or the "Global Recession of 2009."

I think examining that ten year period is extremely valuable, since it includes some good times and a very bad period as well.

What I didn't say before was that when the recession started in December, 2007, the hypothetical $10,000 you had originally invested in the Fidelity Spartan 500 Index Fund in 2004 would have grown to $14,149. By Feb. 28, 2009, the value fell to $7,284, a 48% drop over 14 months. (Gasp!)

If you panicked and sold you'd have a 48% loss, compared to the time the recession started.

But by standing pat the investment recovered to $22,285 by Aug. 31, 2014.

Dad knows people who panic when the market goes down. "They sell. Big mistake. Then they don't buy until the prices recover. Another big mistake. Backwards."

Dad tells me, "You invested in good companies. Just because the stock price goes down one day it doesn't mean the company is really less valuable. The company is still there doing business like it was the day before."

A lot of business was impacted by the recession. But every one of those companies scrambled to recover. And your $10,000 hypothetical investment grew.

Relax!

## 4.19.  Keeping Up with the Market

Now that you're invested in the market you may be inclined to read *The Wall Street Journal* or watch financial news networks on cable TV.

Great!

But don't get too excited. (Or depressed.)

---

*The news media makes money by getting readership and viewers and selling ads. To keep you interested and tuned in, they have to keep you excited. That means they highlight bad news and focus on the sensational. That's okay for them, but not so good for you as you make decisions about your investments.*

---

I remember working as a newspaper reporter when I was in college. I went out to cover a tornado that hit Garden City, Kan. Did we take pictures of the town in general? No, we photographed the most spectacular damage and ran those pictures in the newspaper.

Why? Because people wanted to see the tornado damage. They didn't want to see all the undamaged parts of town.

It makes sense, when you think about it.

But when you start to get financial market news, you need to remain aware that there's a *bias for the sensational*. This is true even on market analysis shows, where they try to analyze and predict the market. (Which they can't do, because no one can.) That's okay, but *don't start making investment decisions based on it*.

### 4.19.1.  *Watching Financial News on TV*

"My take is to be exposed to financial news all the time, so you can wink at it," suggests financial advisor Joshua Brown. "Then when you hear a prediction that scares people, you can say, 'Yeah, I hear stuff like that every day, and it never matters.' That's how you deal with the noise.

"It's not abnormal for the stock market to be going up. It's normal," Brown says in an interview by Pat Regnier for *Money* (Oct., 2014). "Here's a fun fact. Fifty years of history, pick any day of the month of any year going back, and it turns out you have a 75% chance of the market being higher one year later."

Whether you watch financial news on TV or get it on your smartphone, take it all as entertainment, not as actionable information. I quote Jim Cramer in this letter, but he's a champion of sensationalizing the purchase of individual stocks. Just relax and stick with mutual funds.

I enjoy checking on my investments regularly. I keep up with what's happening; I like that.

You'll also find me groaning when I see the markets go down.

If they go down too much, I stop checking. In fact, there have been some *years* when I've not checked my investments except to glance at the year-end statements I received from Fidelity.

Some of those years were times of big gains; I'd have been excited if I had been watching.

---

*When you have a solid long-term investment strategy you don't have to watch the markets every day, or check on your investment results.*
*Just let the fund managers do their jobs.*

---

## 4.20. Should You Ever Sell?

If your financial plan is a buy and hold strategy, should you ever sell a mutual fund or stock you've bought?

Yes, but it shouldn't happen often. Since you're investing in mutual funds, you may be concerned about the managers who determine which stocks to buy. Investment houses like Fidelity and Vanguard work very hard to avoid issues when managers change, but it does happen.

If you are notified that the name of the fund is changing, or the investment objectives are changing, or the manager is changing, you want to watch a fund carefully.

Clearly, if a fund is changing it hopes to do better, but if those changes do not align with your sector decisions, you may want to move that money to another fund.

Also, watch the Morningstar ratings. Remember how I told you to choose a fund with a four-star or five-star rating? If it goes down below that, it's because Morningstar sees new risk. That, alone, doesn't mean you should sell, but it means you should watch what's happening with the fund.

If you become concerned about a fund, watch what companies they buy, and watch the returns relative to the S&P 500. Any sector fund you choose should grow faster than the S&P 500 grows. It may also drop more than the S&P 500 during downtimes. That's normal.

---

*You should also revisit your decisions about the sectors you want to buy.*
*If a sector fund quits producing, maybe it's because*
*that sector no longer has a future.*

---

If you sell be sure to reinvest into a sector fund that you've investigated and expect to do well.

Jason Hall of *Motley Fool* says his biggest regret happened twice in his 20s when he cashed out retirement accounts, worth a combined $6,500. "Replacing $6,500 today would be easy," he says, but the additional money generated by investing? "Coming up with an extra hundred grand in retirement? Not so much. I'm just glad I figured this out before I ran out of time." (*CNNMoney*, "My Biggest Investing Regret," May 28, 2015)

## 4.21. Rebalancing Your Portfolio

If you're following Strategy A and your portfolio consists of just one fund, your S&P 500 Index tracking fund, no rebalancing is necessary. It automatically stays balanced.

But with a Strategy B portfolio you might think about rebalancing it from time to time. Or you might not. Let me explain.

Over time with several different funds in your portfolio, you will find that some perform better than others. In fact, some will probably perform much better than the others.

The result is that even though you followed the strategy to the letter and put equal amounts into Fund A, Fund B, and Fund C, market growth in sectors has resulted in you having a lot more value in one or more funds.

Suppose Fund A was a big winner and has three times the value as your investment in Funds B and C.

Some advisors would tell you that you're now overexposed in that sector and should rebalance your investment so A, B, and C are more equally invested. (You would sell some of A and reinvest it in B and C.) The idea would be to keep the $40% - 20% - 20% - 20% mix, even as fund values change.

Other advisors would say continue to hold; if one sector has rewarded you then you should let it continue to grow.

Which is the best approach?

Frankly, both are valid ideas. The conservative approach would be to rebalance. The aggressive approach would be to hope that a winning sector would continue its higher growth rate. (In fact, it might, or it might not.)

There's no perfect answer. I'm inclined to hold, however, and here's why:

We are not talking about holding a stock; instead, we're holding a sector-specific mutual fund. If the fund is holding too much of any one stock, the fund managers should rebalance and adjust for that. So you should already be balanced well within the sector.

Unless you have reason not to invest in that sector, or reason to not trust the fund management, you should be safe to hold.

We already discussed the situations where you should sell. If you should be selling, sell, don't just rebalance.

What if the sector goes into a correction phase and goes down? Relax. You're invested broadly in the general market (with your S&P 500 Index tracking fund) and you're invested in three different sectors. You're pretty well diversified. Let the winners continue to win.

Note that this applies to our mutual fund strategy, not to stock investing.

# 5. Living the Wealth Builder Lifestyle

Part of the investing picture is having money to invest, that is, fitting your spending plan to your income so you really can pay yourself first with 30% of your paycheck.

In this section, I'll be covering ideas to help you with that, and, in the process, building some more of that Wealth Builder mindset that is so necessary for this to work. Once this is working, you can actually start investing and that's covered in the next section.

## 5.1. Managing Your Money – Spending

You're going to invest money, and you're going to spend money, of course.

In *The Millionaire Next Door* the point is made that millionaires are frugal. They spend cautiously and never lose sight of the idea that they are building wealth.

Frugality is a major reason Wealth Builders are wealthy.

Block any inclination to adopt the high consumption lifestyle that many of your friends and neighbors exhibit.

---

*Your success in accumulating wealth lies in living well below your means and investing the difference for compound earnings.*

---

Our financial plan allocates 30% of your paycheck to investments, including your Protection Fund for unexpected expenses. That leaves 70% to spend. For all I say about being frugal, remember you get 70% to spend.

### 5.1.1.  *Track Your Money and File Your Receipts*

Use a check register or small notebook to track every expenditure, from your bank account to your cash.

Tracking will help you in two ways:

* You will learn where your money goes.
* You will be discouraged from spending because you won't want to report irrational purchases, even to yourself.

By far, the most important is knowing where your money goes. This simple record becomes your scorecard as you lead your financial life.

When you get a receipt for a purchase, any purchase, file it where you can find it later. I like to use what's called an expanding file for this; you can find one at any office supply store. Get one with 12 or 13 sections, and label a section for each month of the year.

As you get receipts, just stuff them in the current month's slot. Very easy.

Now you can look back at a month's receipts and know where the money went.

And if you need a receipt for a return or a tax record, it will be handy and relatively easy to find.

## 5.2.  Expenses or Investments?

Think a moment about how you use your money.

Most of what we use money for is expenses. Food, clothing, household goods, transportation, books, entertainment, jewelry, and rent are all expenses.

Sometimes I get some resistance on this. I've heard things like:

"I invest in good clothing because it helps me make a good impression on the job." Yes, but have you been to a yard sale lately? The resale value of clothing is virtually nothing! Some really expensive clothing may sell at a consignment shop, but at a big discount and you give a lot to the store. It might not sell. And it's a hassle. What's it really worth?

"When I buy furniture for my home I consider that a good investment." Your banker may allow some of that on your balance sheet, but, again, have you been to a garage sale lately? That $1,200 sofa is on sale for $25 and may not sell at that price!

"My jewelry is a good investment." Fine jewelry is probably a better investment than clothing and furniture, but if you have the stomach for a reality check, take your most expensive piece of jewelry to a pawn shop and see what you can get for it. Depressed? Take it back to the store where you bought it and see what they will offer you. Not much difference.

Jewelry, art, and other collectibles may actually rise in value if you allow enough time but they will be hard to sell and you will give up most of the value to the jewelry store or gallery who sells it.

What about your car? Cars are expensive and lose value as soon as you buy them. The value goes down each year. Insurance and repairs are expensive. Fuel and routine maintenance cost money, too.

Is your home an expense or an investment?

"Rent" is a legitimate expense. You need a place to live, whether it's a small apartment or a larger home.

If you are able to stay in one place and you buy your home, you are exchanging rent for a mortgage, taxes, insurance, and repairs. All that is what we would call a "rent factor" and that makes it an expense, just like rent.

Over time, rents go up but your mortgage payment stays the same, and eventually you pay off the mortgage. Your "rent factor" stays the same and ultimately goes down (on payoff)... a big advantage.

One big difference with a home is that when you buy a home and keep it long enough, the value usually grows. There's also a large industry reselling homes so it's usually not hard to sell a home as long as you're not deeply in debt. If you price it reasonably you can turn it to cash within a few months. That's not a liquid investment but it's reasonable.

So a home purchase is both an expense and an investment. Because rent is an expense, we include these outlays in the expense side of your financial plan, not in the wealth building side. But it does build wealth over time and if you plan this right your home will be paid off well before you retire reducing your "rent factor" and giving you more to spend elsewhere.

## 5.2.1. *Black Friday Bargains – Are They?*

I like a good deal as much as anyone, but Black Friday and Cyber Monday were created to get people to spend outrageous sums on things they really don't need by creating fake events.

Hoards of people go from store to store spending with cash and credit cards as if it were the last sale ever! They do this with little regard for actual need or their financial plan (a plan which they probably don't have).

Many people wrongly think they are getting a "deal" by putting up with the crowds. But they are living day to day and getting these deals replaces sanity and planning for a successful life.

Sadly, banks are eager to lend this money with only a little regard for ability to repay. So many people put themselves into endless debt to have simple materialistic items.

Even cash buyers spend freely ignoring the fact that the cash they spend now will become a problem when other bills come due or investments need to be made.

Americans for the most part are broke.

There's nothing wrong with buying things if you have the money and it fits your financial plan. Review your plan and don't get caught up in the buying frenzy.

### 5.2.2. 'Can I Afford That?' – That May Be a Toxic Thought

When we make a major purchase we often ask ourselves, "Can I afford that?"

The answer can be toxic. Here's why...

Suppose you're looking for a new place to rent.

You look around and find three places that are suitable. The only problem: they are all a bit higher than you were planning.

So you start thinking about your other expenses and find some things you can reduce or adjust, and figure you can squeak by with one of the new rentals. You've made your decision; you sign the lease and move in.

The problem is this: You've squeezed everything to make it fit. You probably have not left room for unexpected expenses or setbacks in the number of hours you work or a change in jobs.

When something happens, you're in trouble. And something will happen! It always does!

### 5.2.3. Can Shuffling Expenses Be a Good Thing?

Sure. There are times it makes sense.

When I switched our household over to smartphones, it was a good move. Why? Because I eliminated three telephone landlines that served our home and my consulting business. That cost reduction more than covered the extra cost of upgrading our cell phones.

Shopping for the best cell phone "deal" made a difference, too, switching to a service reseller instead of using one of the big cellular companies. I get the same coverage, and I'm paying half what most of my friends pay for their phone service by doing serious comparison shopping.

The net result was that our total cell phone bill was reduced, plus we eliminated the landlines. Overall, our phone bill was cut to less than half what we paid before.

The difference is that it wasn't a justification for paying more; we actually paid less.

## 5.3. How Does Spending Money Affect Your Future?

Remember that chart that showed how much your money would grow when invested, compounding the returns?

---

*Each time you spend money, it costs you in the future.*

---

For example, if you have a $3,500 whopper car repair, it costs you $616,955 of 40-year later money! (That's 176,273 x 3.5 = 616,955.)

Smaller expenses have an equal, if smaller, effect.

If you buy a new, larger TV set for $1,500, it costs you $264,409.

I'm older and time is running shorter, but even a ten-year analysis makes one think.

That $3,500 car repair costs me $12,750 ten years in the future. The $1,500 TV costs me $5,464 in future money.

I'd like to think I have a lot more than ten years left, and I'd like to continue building wealth.

Of course, you have to repair the car, so I hope you have planned for auto repairs and have the funds for it in your 70% or as excess funds invested in your Protection Fund. The TV? Maybe you should wait for that, especially if it's not in your financial plan.

When you buy things, being frugal generally means not buying the fancy model of something with all the bells and whistles. Instead buy the basic model.

Will this disappoint you? A study by the *Journal of Consumer Research* shows that most people are actually happier with the basic model of a product; it's easier to use, there's less to learn, and less to break.

### 5.3.1. *Going on Vacation*

Sometimes you really *need* a vacation.

You know I love to go to Disneyland.

I don't go to Disneyland as often as I'd like, however, because it doesn't fit in my financial plan. I've even cancelled trips to Disneyland at the last minute because it didn't fit the financial plan.

---

*I wanted to go to Disneyland when I was seven years old, the year Disneyland opened. My parents didn't take me because it wasn't in their financial plan. We went camping in a borrowed tent in Colorado because Colorado was nearby and camping was cheap. I joke about that today (poor me!), but it was an important financial lesson.*

---

I didn't get to Disneyland until I was 38 years old and I was already across the street at the Anaheim Convention Center for a business meeting. I extended my stay for a day and went to Disneyland.

I've also been fortunate by writing books and giving speeches about my Disneyland experiences; I've actually been paid (indirectly) for going to Disneyland. Most people can't do that.

So... what do you do when you really need a vacation?

Look at your financial plan and decide what you can afford without breaking the plan.

A Disneyland trip is expensive. Does it fit in your 70%? Have a great trip!

If it doesn't fit, think about staying in a near-to-home budget hotel for a getaway and hiking in the country. Or, like my parents, camping in a not-so-distant camping area.

And while you're there, take a bit of that time to think about the fact that you're on the road to building wealth!

"But, Grandaddy, we really love Disneyland!"

I know. Me, too. But figure out how to afford that trip from your 70%. And when you do go on vacation, take a minute to enjoy the experience realizing you're also building wealth.

> *As much as we love going out to eat, or seeing the hot new movie in theaters, or having 900 HD channels at our disposal, the fact is that all of those things are ultimately useless, and very pricey.*
>
> *If you want to climb out of debt, you'll need to put your money toward doing so, and not on frivolous ventures.*
>
> *So cut back on everything not necessary for survival – cook your own food as much as you can, wait for movies to appear on Netflix, cancel all but basic cable – and start taking debt slashing seriously.*
>
> *You can still have fun with life, but it doesn't have to cost a ton.*
>
> *– Mary Hiers, personal finance writer, mint.com.*

## 5.4.  You *Will* Have Unexpected Bills

You *will* have unexpected bills. I promise.

An unexpected bill is any expense that you didn't expect. That sounds obvious, but so often I hear people complain something like, "My car needed a $3,500 repair and there was no way I could have expected that!"

No, but you can plan on having unexpected bills. You just don't know what it will be. Maybe it's an unexpected hot water heater replacement, an air conditioner repair, or a roof repair.

I refer you back to your Protection Account. Invest enough in there to cover three years income, plus money for these emergencies.

If you keep investing there, eventually you should have enough that the growth in that account covers all these unexpected bills and has some left over!

## 5.5.   Drive a Safe, Practical Car

Washington Redskins running back Alfred Morris has a four-year, $2.2 million contract. AARP tells us he "still drives his 1991 Mazda nicknamed 'Bentley,' which he reportedly purchased for $2 from his pastor when he was a student at Florida Atlantic University."

In 2004 I cleverly bought a new Toyota Prius. It's a comfortable car and we put over 125,000 miles on it. Around town we got 46 miles per gallon, saving lots of gas money. It seemed very practical; I like getting mileage that's well above average.

Nine years later, granddaughter Kysa has that car. Shortly after she started driving it the battery died, a $3,500 repair. That's an extra 2.8 cents a mile, times 46 miles per gallon... or about $1.28 per gallon. The battery replacement cost is like paying $1.28 a gallon extra for gas.

It's not so practical after all. I've owned two hybrids, but I'm not so keen on them now.

My next car was a Volkswagen diesel. Sometimes diesel is a little more expensive than gasoline but nowhere near $1.28 more. I still get amazing mileage (as much as 53mpg on the highway) and I don't have an expensive battery replacement in my future.

Not long ago granddaughter Rachel bought a used Volkswagen Passat. She bought it from a doctor who had driven it for 10 years. It's a nice looking car, and will serve her well for a time.

She would rather have a convertible. So would I, but that's not very practical.

A fancy car might encourage thieves to steal it or follow you home to burglarize your house.

A fancy car might cause contractors to bid home repair jobs higher.

A fancy car might bring resentment to fellow employees, including those who work with you and those who work for you.

When you buy a used car, like Rachel's Passat, you know you're getting someone else's problems. You're getting a car that's not just older but will have some repair issues. You have to plan that into the budget and remember you got a car for half (or less) of the new car price.

I know you probably won't find a two-dollar bargain like Alfred Morris. But paying cash for a used car that's affordable and keeping it 10 years will keep you from becoming car-poor.

Is it okay to buy a car on payments? Yes, if you get a low interest rate and if the payment fits into your spending plan as part of the 70% of take-home pay. A three-year loan is the longest you should get. (Yes, I know a lot of people get six year car loans; you should not.)

Never get a lease. (Dealers love to sell you a lease because they make a lot of extra money on a lease. That's *your* money.)

Car payments, along with insurance, fuel, and maintenance, are an ongoing item in your spending plan for the rest of your life. I hope someday you have extra funds in your Protection Account that you can use to buy a car without payments!

## 5.6.   Should You Rent or Buy a Home?

"Cheap housing is your new BFF," says Heather Long, writing for *CNNMoney* (May 26, 2015). She recommends keeping your rent-factor below 25% of your salary, good advice whether you rent or buy. "...the reality for most recent grads is that your rent payment will determine whether you financially flourish or flunk."

The 25% rent-factor applies at any age, though your goal by retirement is to own your home *and* have it fully paid off.

## 5.7.   When to Buy a House

It was Jen's dream to own her own home. My neighbor, Jen (not her real name), found a home in our neighborhood and the real estate agent introduced her to a mortgage banker who "can help you get the home you want." Jen paid too much; the market was high.

The mortgage banker qualified her purchase and encouraged Jen to finance with payments she could not afford. (It's silly for bankers to promote loans that may not be paid back, but they do. You must use common sense and figure it out for yourself. You can't trust the banker.)

The real estate agent made a big commission. The mortgage banker made a big commission. Jen didn't fare so well.

Jen is left with a mortgage she can barely pay, home repairs that she cannot afford, a home worth less than she paid for it, and her savings gone.

Jen is lucky; many homeowners who bought during that period of time lost their homes, with credit ruined, savings depleted, and still on the hook for the loss on the sale of the home.

### 5.7.1.   Should You Ever Buy a House?

Sure, it may be one of the best investments you can make because it goes up in value (hopefully) and it saves you rent.

If you pay rent to a landlord all your life, at the end of your life you'll have nothing to show for it. If you instead pay a mortgage on a house, at the end of your life you'll have a house to show for it. Own your own home, and pay off the mortgage early so when you retire (or before) your rent factor is reduced to zero.

But there are times not to buy.

### 5.7.2.   How to Buy a House

Buy for the right reasons.

**Location, location, and location**. In real estate, they like to say the three most important things about selling a property are location, location, and location.

Location is an important factor for you, too. But for you it's not the only factor.

78

**Buy when your debt situation is right**. Some counselors will suggest you shouldn't buy if you have any debt, but that's not reasonable. After all, whether you're buying a home or paying rent, you have a cash cost for housing. But don't buy if you have any credit card or other high-interest debt. Pay that off first. A car payment shouldn't stop you from buying a home, but the car payment *and* the mortgage payment should fit into your spending plan as part of the 70% of your take-home pay.

**Buy when you won't be moving soon**. The best home ownership strategy would be to buy a home and stay in it for the rest of your life. That probably won't be practical, but like with other investments, it's time that works the magic for you so the longer you stay in the home the more value it has for you.

**Buy when the market is *not* high**. You'll never know if the market is at its low point (until it's too late), but you can get an idea about real estate prices in your area from the news. If they're high, they will probably cycle down in a year or two. Don't make Jen's mistake. Wait for a better time to buy.

**Buy when you can find the right home**. Find a nice home that will serve you and your family for a number of years and the combined payments for mortgage, insurance, taxes, and a maintenance allowance do not exceed what you pay for rent.

Lots of folks move every four or five years. When you buy a home it should be someplace you expect to stay for 10 or 20 years, well past the time you've paid off the mortgage. That means you want to strategize your career so moving isn't part of the plan.

**Buy a home so the payment is no more than 25% of your take-home pay**. This is a long-standing guideline for home buyers, but it's often forgotten in the excitement of new home ownership.

**Buy when you can get a good mortgage rate**. Mortgage rates change from time to time, and you don't want to get saddled with a high rate. Don't get finicky with this; some people get worried about buying this week or next week because the rates might change. It's more important to watch how rates are this year compared to other years.

Your house payment, which includes taxes and insurance, needs to fit into your spending plan as part of the 70% of take-home pay. It's a rent-factor. In addition, as a homeowner you'll have to pay for things you don't have to cover when you were renting, like repairs and maintenance. Sometimes these can get expensive. And there are always some of these expenses, almost all unexpected, so add some to your rent-factor to include an allowance for that.

### 5.7.3. *What Kind of Financing?*

As I write this 15-year mortgage rates are about 3%. Since 1971 rates have varied from 2.66% to 18.45%. Financing a home between 1979 and 1985 would have been at rates over 10%. That's way too high and resulted in massive refinancing activity as rates went down and homeowners tried to get new financing on their existing homes at lower rates. This resulted in more big commissions for the mortgage bankers, the only real winners in this situation.

A 15-year mortgage brings the lowest payment so get that. Never get an *ARM*, or *Adjustable Rate Mortgage*. It sounds like a great rate to start, and it is, but you don't really know what you'll be paying.

Then use a mortgage calculator program to calculate how much you would have to pay each month to *pay it off in ten years*, not 15. Take that amount, add the allowance for taxes and insurance, and that's your monthly payment amount.

Since there's no penalty for prepayment, you can add to the payment every month and pay off the loan much earlier. This will save you thousands of dollars in interest.

*Remember interest? It's that charge the banks use to make themselves wealthy. You want to reverse that game as fast as possible.*

You need to be able to afford your new home, without tapping your wealth accounts.

If you're thinking of buying a home, you'll need a down payment, ideally at least 20% of the purchase price. (That may be hard to do and there are ways to reduce that to 10 or 15%. The mortgage banker can help with this.) Start putting money aside, investing it in a special account so you'll have it when you are ready to buy.

### 5.7.4. *Refinancing and Second Mortgages*

**Rate reduction refinancing**. If you get a mortgage with a high rate of interest and then rates go down, you may be tempted to "refinance" your home at the new, lower rate and get a lower monthly payment. Even though you get a lower payment, you can continue to make the same payment and pay off your home even faster.

This may be a great idea, but there are a couple of caveats:

First, you may be tempted to increase the amount of the loan. Don't give in to this temptation. You want this loan paid off as fast as possible, and that won't happen if you refinance and it increases the amount you owe.

A lot of people see this as an opportunity to get money for a vacation or for remodeling. Instead, as a Wealth Builder you want to pay off the loan as fast as possible, which will leave more in your spending budget for other things.

Second, some folks see this as a chance to increase the length of payments from the time that's left to another full 15 years or longer. Resist this temptation, too, again because you want to pay this off as fast as possible.

**Getting a second mortgage**. Lenders are often willing to loan you more money, either by refinancing your mortgage or by making a second loan using your home as security. A second mortgage is usually made at a higher interest rate, and the banker focuses on whether you can afford the payments rather than on how much more interest you'll be paying.

Why? Because bankers like to make more money.

But your task is to get out of debt and to pay it all off as quickly as possible. Pass on the second mortgage.

### 5.7.5.  *The Advantages of Home Ownership*

Often, your home value appreciates. That means the investment value goes up; you can sell for more than you paid.

Over time your housing cost should stay level, even while rental rates are climbing. At that point you are actually saving rent money.

---

*Long before you retire you want to have your home completely paid off, so you're only paying insurance, taxes, and maintenance. It becomes a paid-up asset on your personal balance sheet.*

---

In *The Millionaire Next Door*, Stanley suggests this rule for determining how much to mortgage when buying a home:

*If you're not yet wealthy but want to be someday, never purchase a home that requires a mortgage loan that is more than twice your household's total annual realized income.*

Be aware that the mortgage broker will probably show you that you are qualified for a higher mortgage. Don't be flattered. A bigger mortgage is in his interest, not yours. (He earns a commission; the more you pay in interest and fees, the more he makes.)

There *are* less expensive neighborhoods to consider for your new home ownership.

### 5.7.6.  *Buying a Second Home*

Let me tell you about one couple, the son of a close friend who married his best friend from his childhood. They have a great relationship. Each has a good job, so they have a very nice combined income. And they've been building savings.

They're under 30 and thinking of buying a second home in Mexico. They have no children, so expenses are low, and they figure they can afford it. After all, they have to spend it somewhere.

Somehow, they've also been led to believe it's a good investment. I can't pass judgment on that, but I know they will be tying up money in an investment that's likely to be hard to sell and will involve future costs including taxes, maintenance, and insurance.

### 5.7.7. *Timeshares*

At some point you'll get the "opportunity" to invest in a timeshare, your part-time share of a vacation property that promises to save you money on vacations for decades with a simple investment and small annual or monthly maintenance fee.

Don't be tricked! They often offer free or discounted vacations in return for listening to the "short" sales presentation. During that sales presentation, typically several hours long, they will try *very hard* to convince you to buy. (The salespeople are highly motivated to sell you. My friend, Rick, did this for awhile and told me they earn a fat commission when you buy and get fired if you don't. That's why they push you so hard to buy.)

It's a great deal for the real estate developer. They sell a condo worth, say $500,000, for two and one-half times as much… or more. And they still get to make money on the maintenance fees which are likely to increase each year.

If I haven't convinced you and you are thinking of buying anyway, check the resale market and buy your timeshare from someone other than the original promoter. You'll probably find a substantial discount, which will save some money… and which illustrates how much the value drops and how hard it is to sell this kind of investment.

## 5.8. Marrying Right

Contrary to the story in the romance movies, love isn't everything.

As I grew older I saw that children in wealthy families often married children from other wealthy families. The marriage was more than a personal partnership, it was the marriage of two families of wealth, increasing the family wealth for both families. A few generations back, marriages were arranged by the parents and that's why; parents wanted to be sure their children married into a family that would create a partnership of sorts between the families.

Even families with moderate assets tried to marry their children to someone from a family of equal or higher position.

We don't do that so much today, and I think wealth isn't everything. But there is an important factor that remains crucial.

---

*Find a partner who wants to be a Wealth Builder.*

---

I did pretty well because I married someone who championed me and supported me in all that I could do. She also champions the concept of building wealth and growing investments. That's good.

It's likely the most important factor.

If your partner wants to be a Wealth Builder, like you do, you can embark on the adventure together. You may have discussions about where to invest, and what funds are providing the better earnings.

But you won't have a partner who wants to spend everything you earn; that can destroy your efforts to build wealth.

### 5.8.1.  *Elaborate Weddings*

I read in *USA Today* that the average American wedding now costs $31,213, not including the honeymoon. That's a lot! (Eric McWhinnie, The Cheat Sheet, for *USA Today* May 2, 2015)

Using the $176,000 factor, that's worth $5,493,488 in 40 years, so the average wedding is worth over five million dollars in retirement money.

That's not to say you shouldn't have a nice wedding, but think a bit about what it really costs. A five million dollar retirement investment is a pretty nice wedding present. McWhinnie says, "A wedding is meant to be a celebration of love, not a hindrance to financial prosperity."

I met a young woman not long ago who was planning her wedding. She didn't want to hear this message. Maybe she was marrying a man who is already financially independent. (I doubt it.)

## 5.9.  Spending Right

Nearly a third of U.S. households earning $75,000 a year live check-to-check some of the time according to a survey released in 2015 by SunTrust.

Eating out, entertainment, and other discretionary items make up most of their overspending.

Even earning 50% more than the median household income doesn't mean they manage their money well. As I've pointed out repeatedly, the important thing is to learn to be a frugal spender.

I'm going to cover a number of areas where you might be able to cut spending, though some might seem severe. I'm not trying to tell you to do *all* this, but consider each tip as an opportunity that might help you build wealth.

What you actually spend will depend on how much you have in your 70%, right?

Whatever your income, always live below your means.

And remember that frugal living is a habit that will pay you for years.

### 5.9.1. *Eating At Home and Other Culinary Delights*

As I noted, eating out is one of the top areas of overspending.

Their kitchens and budgets may be more expansive than yours, but many celebrities prefer to cook at home rather than dine out at fancy five-star restaurants. AARP shares that Selena Gomez, Taylor Swift and Emma Stone enjoy getting together for baking parties at each other's homes.

You think that on your budget a trip to McDonald's or Wendys is okay? Eating at home still saves you money, and it adds up fast. How do you think those restaurants pay for all their staff and facilities? By including those costs – and profits – in the price.

---

*Eating at home doesn't mean you have to become a slave in the kitchen, either. There are plenty of easy-to-prepare meals that you'll find at the grocery store that can be fixed in minutes.*

---

Planning ahead makes this easy. If you go to the refrigerator or cupboard and don't find food you like, you'll think you need to go to the store, and while you're out anyway, you'll be back with fast food getting an inferior meal at a higher price.

Throwing out unwanted snacks and meals costs you hundreds of dollars each year, too. A bit of meal planning, and freezing leftovers, is like finding money!

Soft drinks, chips, and candy may be delicious but they injure your health, increase consumption of non-beneficial food, and cost more than you think.

Making rounds to Starbucks or other coffee shops? If you regularly buy coffee through the week, you're spending over a thousand bucks a year on coffee. Save that for special occasions and fire up your Mr. Coffee.

### 5.9.2. *Entertainment*

We already discussed going on vacation. But what about that daily entertainment expense?

### 5.9.2.1. *Cable TV*

My cousin, Ken, has sworn off cable TV. "TV is free," he says. "I get 12 local channels; that's plenty." Even in smaller towns in Kansas, free TV provides a lot of entertainment. (Yes, big towns have free TV, too.)

Every time I tell this story, I get an objection. "But I'd miss out on ESPN," or "I can't live without my HBO." Think about that. Has your life come to the point that a film on HBO or a sporting event on ESPN defines your most important entertainment?

Am I telling you to drop cable? No. I'm trying to get you to *think about what you really need* rather than just doing what you've always done. A cable bill of $70 - $150 a month adds up to $840 - $1,800 a year. Over 40 years, we're talking 40 to 60 thousand dollars; if you *invested* it that cable money would be worth two million or more.

Cable packages can add $15 to $20 a month per premium channel. Multiply that times 12 to get an annual rate. Over 40 years, invested, you're talking nearly $25,000. Is HBO worth *that?*

If you have broadband internet, you can add Amazon Prime or Netflix for substantially less and get a lot of additional entertainment for not much money.

### 5.9.2.2. *Internet*

Not long ago I ran into a friend who had trouble getting internet in her home. She needed it only for email and limited internet browsing. Cable internet wasn't an option so she added a broadband hot spot to her too expensive cell phone plan and for $20 a month solved her problem.

Shopping around you may find a better price for a similar service. The major wireless companies resell their service through others where you can often get a better price. It pays to check. I showed her another vendor who would supply 500MB a month for free, enough for her use. You probably don't need the fastest internet available; your effective speed also depends on the other end of your internet connection and those seldom match the highest speed cable internet offerings.

### 5.9.2.3. *Movies*

Have you looked at the price of a movie lately? Is there a discount theatre near you? For less than half the "regular" price, we go to the discount theatre to see the same films a few weeks later on the big screen. If we go on the right day, it's even cheaper as they have a bargain day where tickets are a dollar less and popcorn is discounted.

### 5.9.3. *Online Purchasing*

I'm often able to buy things online from Amazon or another reputable vendor at a savings. Shipping is often free.

Just don't get caught up in the idea of buying things; only buy what you need. Dave Ramsey, money management expert, says amazing amounts are spent on deal websites and home shopping channels for unneeded and useless merchandise.

Paying for speedy shipping to get your purchase as soon as possible burns up savings in an instant, so use bargain shipping.

### 5.9.4.  *Tobacco*

When I was eight years old, I made a decision not to smoke cigarettes when I was older because they cost *25 cents a pack*, and it seemed to me my parents wasted a lot of money on cigarettes. (Yes, at eight years old  I figured out they were spending $360 a year on cigarettes.) I stuck by that decision, reinforced by health concerns. Today, of course, cigarettes cost a *lot more* and it's a significant expense. (My parents quit smoking when I was 13.)

We're real proud of Brian for quitting cigarettes, and I think he's also discovered there's a financial benefit in addition to the health benefits.

*USA Today* (March 24, 2014) reports 14 percent of Americans' incomes are spent on cigarettes. That's crazy!

### 5.9.5.  *Alcohol*

Alcohol is another expensive choice. That same story in *USA Today* said the average American consumer spends one percent of all spending on alcohol. Restaurants and bars have increased their alcohol pricing.

I'm no teetotaler, but I generally limit myself to a few glasses of wine a month rather than making it a daily routine or thirst quenching part of meals or activities.

I'm pretty careful where I get those glasses of wine, too. I have a friend who bought a bottle of wine to serve the table in a nice restaurant on a cruise ship, and it cost $250. It was a gracious gift and a delightful dinner. The same brand and vintage is available locally for $16. I expect a nice restaurant to mark up the price, but that's ridiculous.

Water is the best thirst-quencher, and doctors will tell you few people drink enough water.

### 5.9.6.  *Wasted Energy*

Saving energy seems like an impossible challenge, but it turns into dollars. Energy Star says consumers can cut energy expense by a third by using the recommendations and suggestions on their website checklist.

Your electric utility company probably has suggestions as well. Check their website and check inserts with utility bills.

### 5.9.7.  *Speeding and Traffic Tickets*

When I was working with the photo radar companies, I was amazed at how high fines are when you get caught speeding. (Officer-issued tickets are just as expensive.)

It varies depending on location and offense, but the average cost in the United States is $150 (including court fees). In Arizona, it starts around $250 for 10 miles per hour over and goes up from there. Your insurance company may raise your insurance rates, too.

When I was in college my friend, Jeff, said he figured that if he drove 15 miles an hour over the speed limit he might get to his destination three or four minutes earlier, even though it seems faster. Is it worth it? Jeff didn't think so.

### 5.9.8.  *Designer Clothing*

Trendy clothes from the hot stores can be expensive. If you have the money, fine, but when you're trying to be frugal, shop the discount outlet stores and match up a trendy shirt or top with more generic pants.

Some consignment stores and thrift stores can be a good source, too.

What about children's clothes? Parents all want their babies and children to look beautiful, but expensive designer clothing is a bad way to spend money. It's amazing how much some of these items cost. Kids outgrow shoes and clothes quickly.

### 5.9.9.  *Shopping Sales and Stocking Up*

Shopping sales may save you money, but only if you're buying something you use regularly and will continue to use.

If your favorite canned soup is on sale at the grocery store for half price, by all means, stock up! But don't buy flavors or varieties that aren't your favorite; those will sit on the shelf and are a waste of your money. Don't stock up on perishables, either; they may not last.

Think about the investment value when you stock up.

If that soup is normally $3.00, but it's on sale for $1.50, every time you use one of those cans of soup in future weeks it's like you avoided spending $3.00 by spending $1.50 a few weeks earlier. If you invest $1.50 in a can of soup this week, and eat that can of soup (then worth $3.00) in a month, you've doubled your money in a month.

That buck-fifty spent now saves you three bucks a month from now.

Don't stock up too far out, however. You want things to stay fresh and in-date. And you just might get tired of that variety of soup.

## 5.10.  Insurance, Yes, But Not Insurance Poor

There are several kinds of insurance that you must buy, some that you should buy, and some that you shouldn't. Insurance salespeople will want to load you up with insurance, so you want to deal with this one carefully.

### 5.10.1.  *Health Insurance*

We already visited about health insurance when we looked into getting a job.

I remember when a young friend of mine thought it wasn't too important to get health insurance. (At least I figured that's what he thought because he didn't have any; actions speak volumes.) Finally he found a job where health insurance was part of the package and it has paid off as his family has had a run of health issues.

Health problems are really expensive, and it's important to be ready to cover the costs. You must have insurance.

Be aware that even with insurance, not all costs will be covered. Of course, you pay for the insurance. In addition to that there are co-pays and expenses that are not covered and you have to pay for that. Plan on it.

### 5.10.2. *Auto Insurance*

There are laws that require you to have insurance on your automobiles, and this is a good thing. Your car is a substantial investment, and it's a risk driving it; an accident can injure you or others as well as damage their property.

As you get older auto insurance premiums will go down, and they will go down the longer you drive without having accidents. Safe driving pays off many ways.

Sticking with the same insurance company is likely to pay off as well with discounts for being a long-term customer. And there's often a discount for insuring your cars and your home with the same insurance company.

Insurance is competitive, so it pays to compare prices from time to time, but I've found that the company I'm with always has the lowest price. Maybe that's because they've insured me for over 40 years.

I get a kick out of the ads that say, "Those that switch to us save an average of $700." How about those that compared prices but didn't switch? How much did they save by not switching?

### 5.10.3. *Homeowners/Renters Insurance*

When you own a home you need insurance to cover loss from fire and theft, and to protect you against lawsuits from those who may be injured on your property. The contents of your home are also covered. (When you finance your home, the mortgage company will require insurance.)

If you're renting do you need coverage? That depends on the value of your personal property, including furniture. I had a college friend who rented and there was a fire in his apartment, destroying all of his and his wife's belongings. They had coverage and their insurance adjuster became their best friend, writing a check to replace nearly everything.

### 5.10.4. *Umbrella Policy*

As you are just starting out you won't need this, but when your assets start to grow you want to protect them from lawsuits, so you need extra insurance. You could increase the coverage of each policy you have, but there's a better solution. Get an umbrella policy.

An umbrella policy covers you above the limits of your homeowners and auto policy, kicking in the extra if those policies don't have enough coverage.

It also covers certain claims that may be excluded by the standard policies including false arrest, libel, and slander.

In effect, it boosts your $300,000 auto liability policy and your $100,000 homeowners liability policy to one or two million dollars coverage, or more.

Remember the idea about keeping your wealth a secret?

There are people who target wealthy families, creating situations where they can sue for a lot of money. They may come to your property and "fall," sustaining injury. I've even heard of crooks who are hurt while breaking into a home turning around and suing the homeowners because they were injured. It doesn't seem fair, does it?

If you're in a car accident and the other party goes to an attorney, the first thing they will do is run a credit check on you to see if it looks like they can get money. Attorneys learned long ago that you sue the people with the money.

If no one knows you're wealthy, that's *some* protection. But if that fails, you want an insurance company ready to protect you. That's what the umbrella policy does.

### 5.10.5. *Whole Life Insurance, No; Term, Yes.*

Life insurance salesmen can paint a pretty dire picture of what happens to your family if you die, and, while some of that picture is true, the product they would really like to sell you is called whole life.

You don't want "whole life insurance." It's a combination of insurance and an investment, and it's a very poor investment. Over the years, insurance companies have paid salespeople really big commissions on whole life because it's so profitable for them. Sometimes the first-year commissions are more than the first-year premium payment, so you know they're expecting big profits from your premiums in future years.

There may be a use for life insurance, especially while your children are living at home. After that, you should have enough in investments and your home should be paid down to the point that you have a low requirement for insurance.

When you do buy life insurance, you want "term life." It's much less expensive because it's pure insurance; there's no investment component. Typically, premiums rise every five or ten years, but because you won't need it when you're older that's okay.

Your employer may include some term life insurance in their benefits package; that's the best place to start. They probably make additional insurance available at a reasonable price; you can compare using online insurance websites.

# 5.11.  Using Credit Cards Wisely

I've already told you that credit is a bad thing, but if you can pay them off each month there may be advantages to using a credit card with a rewards feature.

Every June I have three insurance bills that come due, two auto policies and my homeowners policy. I pay them all with a credit card that gives me 2% back. So my $1,234.72 insurance bill this June resulted in a $24.69 reward that will go into my investment account.

When I fill my car with fuel I'm often able to get a 5% reward. Sixteen gallons at 3.72 means I spent 59.66 and get a 2.98 reward.

These don't sound like earth-shattering rewards, and they're not, but they add up. Each year I'm able to add several hundred dollars to my investment account for buying things I was going to buy anyway!

And don't make the purchase because you get the rebate. I've been watching a national bank advertise their rewards card, suggesting that people should spend more because they get the reward. No! You use the card to get the reward spending money you were already going to spend.

When picking a credit card watch for annual fees (choose one with no annual fee) and caps or limits on special rewards which may be okay but you need to be aware of these limits.

The key is always paying the card off in full each month so you don't get hit with any interest. If you can do that – *no exceptions* – you can find cards that give you the advantage of rewards. Paying interest, typically 13 to 26 percent, kills any advantage.

If I make a big purchase I'll often pay that amount on my card bill right away rather than waiting for a big bill.

If you can't manage to pay these off each month, don't use them.

## *5.11.1.  Credit Card Rules*

1.  Pay your bills in full each month. Typical interest rates of 13-26% are terrible.

2.  Do not spread out your applications. If you're going to apply for two cards, apply for both within two days. It's better for your credit score.

3.  Stay on top of due dates. Never be late. Late fees add up fast, interest is added also, and costs typically exceed any rewards.

4.  Don't use too much credit. Try not to exceed 20-30% of your credit limit.

5.  Track annual fees. It's best to not use cards with annual fees at all, if possible.

---

*Did you know you can pay your credit cards off every week? This is handy if a monthly bill is too big to pay easily. Keep a register of every charge you make on your credit card, just like a checking account register. Total it up every week, and make a payment for that week's charges.*

---

## 5.11.2. A Recent Offer

At some point in your life you will receive offers for credit cards. (I got two in the mail today, and probably average five or six a week.) This is not a compliment, it's a sales pitch. Shred them.

By the way, this is a good reason to have a shredder. It's also a good reason to check your mail every day. I know people who snagged credit card offers from a relative's mailbox, mailed in the applications, and used the cards after they arrived.

That's called *identity theft*. You think you shouldn't have to pay, but this could be a relative, remember? Do you want your relative to go to jail? It can be a very messy situation.

Today I received an offer in the mail with typical terms:

- Annual Percentage Rate (APR) for Purchases: 15.99%, 19.99% or 24.99%, based on your creditworthiness.

- APR for Balance Transfers (Balances you transfer to the card from other cards): 15.99%, 19.99% or 24.99%, based on your creditworthiness.

- APR for Cash Advances: 25.24%

- Penalty APR: Up to 27.24% if you ever pay a credit account late. This often applies even if it's a different account that's paid late.

- Transaction Fees: Balance Transfer: $10 or 3% of the amount of each transfer, whichever is greater.

- Transaction Fees: Cash Advance: $10 or 5% of the amount of each transfer, whichever is greater.

- Penalty Fees: Late Payment or Returned Payment: Up to $35.

Do you see anything in any of these fees that seems reasonable? I don't. A 24.99% APR means that a household with a $15,000 balance will pay $3,750 a year interest. In four years the amount owed will double!

Paying monthly avoids most of the fees. (Some have an annual fee.) Never charge anything you can't pay right away.

### 5.11.3. *Credit Card Checks*

Watch out if you get an offer from your credit card company that includes checks you can deposit in your account or use to pay other bills.

These look enticing, often offering a low interest rate. And they are so easy to use. But there is a catch.

I received one recently and it offered two checks. You could write checks for up to $15,000 with an interest rate of 0% for the first 14 months. That sounds good, but:

There is a 4% fee charged when you write the check. (These typically vary from two to five percent.)

After the 14 months your rate goes up to an astronomical 24.99%.

Payments you make to the account are applied to the promotional balance first, not to other purchases you made with the card. This may vary a bit by offer, but generally means you lose the ability to avoid interest charges by paying for purchases in full.

The best advice: *Shred the checks and avoid these offers.*

## 5.12. And Who Are Your Friends?

Do your friends make a difference?

When I was researching Walt Disney I learned that he surrounded himself at work with talented people who were a big part of Walt's success.

Walt also had successful friends.

Ray Kroc, the guy who made McDonalds into the giant hamburger chain, was a friend Walt met in Red Cross training during World War I.

Fred Gurley, president of the Santa Fe railroad, saw that Walt got VIP treatment when he rode the train to the 1948 Chicago Railroad Fair. Later, his railroad sponsored the Disneyland and Santa Fe Railroad inside Disneyland and Gurley was present at Disneyland's grand opening. The third engine in Disneyland's railroad, added in 1958, was named the Fred Gurley.

Art Linkletter was a successful radio and television host and a business entrepreneur. Linkletter vacationed with Walt and watched as Walt visited Tivoli Gardens, making notes for Disneyland. As Disneyland was being built, Walt took Linkletter to see the progress, then asked him to be the host of the grand opening TV show.

Ward and Betty Kimbell were friends of Walt's. Ward was an animator at the studio and a railroad enthusiast. Ward accompanied Walt on that 1948 trip to the Chicago Railroad Fair, the inspiration for Walt's backyard model railroad and, ultimately, Disneyland.

---

*The people you spend time with are the people whose thoughts you absorb.*
*You become like them.*

---

If you have an old friend from school or from a job who is negative, talks down his job, always seems to have trouble getting a good job, or gets in trouble frequently, distance yourself because you need to protect yourself.

> *"It's better to hang out with people better than you. Pick out associates whose behavior is better than yours and you'll drift in that direction."*
>
> *– Warren Buffett*

## 5.13. Should You Have Your Own Business?

When we started talking about investing, I told you the only way to build real wealth is to own a business. And I said owning a *small business* is usually just buying a glorified job.

I speak from experience. I did it. Don't.

Well, that advice may be a bit severe, even if my 20-20 hindsight thinks it might have been better *for me*.

It's not my intention to stomp on your dream. And *someone* has to become the next Bill Gates. But the likelihood of creating huge success in business is rather small.

---

*When you graduate, everyone tells you the world is yours, you can do*
*anything, even change the world. I agree, but I've come to think you can do it*
*working for someone else.*

---

Owning your own business means you have to deal with *everything* in the business instead of focusing on *your thing* that makes you special.

When I look back I think that I could have worked for someone else and *let them worry* about market conditions, making payroll, cash flow, taxes, opportunity cost, broken toilets, failed air conditioners, and leaky roofs. At the time I thought I had to have my own business.

I could have taken the money I earned at a job and built wealth by buying shares of large companies where someone else would do the work and I would enjoy the profits.

In *The Millionaire Next Door*, Stanley says that many Wealth Builders are self-employed. However, that's misleading, because most people who start a business lose money and close the business within a few years, often spending decades paying off their debt.

Many of those who run a successful business use the same management skills with their investments to build wealth. (Others use their business success to buy things and build debt, resulting in a successful business but a bankrupt owner.)

If you want to be part of "the next new, big thing" hook up with someone else who is doing that and work for them. You'll have a salary, plus a retirement plan and, if it's really the next new, big thing, you'll probably get stock options in the company. If it really does take off, those options may become very valuable.

But that won't happen for most people.

There *is* a special group of self-employed professionals including doctors, attorneys, CPAs, financial planners, and architects, who are able to have a business offering their special services in a small office (or from home) with relatively low overhead. Not everyone in these occupations manages to maintain low overhead, but many do. Remember Jerry Fitch's advice:

*It's not about how much you get, it's about how much you keep.*

If you're going to train for one of these positions, you can work for a company or you can hang out your own shingle. You'll have to be good at marketing your services face-to-face and managing the many aspects of the business while keeping expenses low, in addition to doing the specialized work. And if you're not generating significant income, work for someone else.

You still can invest according to the basic plan I'm describing here, buying your share of big, successful businesses, and participating in the profits.

Most people in the United States are not the entrepreneurial type but they can accumulate considerable wealth through investing while working for someone else.

## 5.14.  Investing in Real Estate

If investing in a home is a good strategy, what about investing in multiple homes and renting them out?

It's not a good idea, because you want to stay *liquid*, which means it's best to have investments in something you can change to cash within a week with little or no hassle. This is not to say you want to cash in your investments, but that day will eventually come and you want it to be easy. That leads us back to the stock market and mutual funds.

Let me tell you Jay's story.

Jay is a family friend who invested in homes and rented them for income. He started with just one home, a home he had lived in but left for a bigger, better home. "Why not rent the old house and make a few bucks?" he reasoned.

Jay did pretty well with that and discovered that he could buy a home on credit, fix it up and rent it to pay off the mortgage.  Over time he did that with a number of homes, each time getting a new mortgage payment. His job ended, but he figured he could make it with his rentals.

Then the housing and banking crash of 2008 hit and Jay's tenants started moving out, leaving him with empty homes that needed repairs, short on cash to make mortgage payments and expenses, and a number of homes whose value had dropped below what he owed so he couldn't afford to sell them.

To top that off, Jay was growing older and really didn't want to have to spend all that effort managing his rentals. He was stuck in a position you don't want to experience. When Jay added it all up, he worried he owed more than the homes were worth and all his hard work had left him with nothing.

Even without the housing market crash, Jay's investment model had several important flaws:

- Buying the homes on credit put him at risk for the payback.

- Renters can be hard to find and even a few months without rent income can put your investment in jeopardy.

- Renters often leave owing back rent and high repair bills well beyond that covered by security deposits.

- Managing rental properties is a tricky process which frequently requires hiring a property manager. That can be expensive, and a bad property manager can spend your money unwisely or steal your funds.

If you think real estate must be your thing, invest in an S&P Real Estate REIT index tracking fund with low expenses; at least you'll have instant liquidity with no debt and someone else can do the heavy lifting. (I looked at that and found other funds that looked like better investments.)

## 5.15. Inheriting Right, or Winning the Lottery

Inheriting and winning the lottery are two ways to get money without earning it. Don't expect it!

Experts say the odds of winning the lottery are less than the odds of getting hit by lightning. You can't count on it.

As to inheriting money, *I'm leaving you this book!* It's worth far more than I can leave you. You can build a lot more wealth than I did. I don't want to spoil any expectations, but I know too many people who expected to inherit money when an uncle, an in-law, a brother, or a parent died, and it turned out there wasn't really anything there for them.

---

*If you do happen into substantial unexpected money, don't blow it. Follow Warren Buffet's plan for his heirs; invest 90% in an S&P 500 Index tracking fund and the remaining 10% in treasury bills or FDIC insured bank CDs.*

---

There will be lots of people courting you for gifts, purchases, and investments, including some, like banks, who seem quite respectable. Just invest it as you've learned here and say, "Sorry, it's all gone." If they press the issue just repeat "Sorry, it's all gone," and hang up the phone.

It's none of their business what you do with your money, and by investing it soundly it really is "gone" in that you can't spend it.

## 5.16. Don't Spoil Your Kids

We all want to give our children (and grandchildren) everything. It's in the nature of parenting, but it can lead to big problems at any age.

The catch is that children who are given too much will fail to learn how to produce for themselves. You want your children to be responsible and to live productive, fulfilling lives. So it's important to teach them how to be productive rather than how to spend a handout.

Does this mean you should never help your children? Of course not. But teaching them how to manage their own lives and letting them do it is the overriding responsibility of parenting.

## 5.17. Don't Cosign for Someone Else's Loans – *Ever!*

One of the most dangerous things you can do is cosign someone else's loan.

The request comes from an adult child, brother, sister, or another loved one who is trying to finance a car, business, home, or something else, or maybe to consolidate all their existing debt. You feel for them and really want to help.

The request always comes in a way that seems so safe. "The bank is happy to loan me what I need to buy this ... but they need you to cosign it. I'll still make all the payments."

The truth is that the bank is *not* willing to loan them that money, but they're happy to loan it to *you*. (The bank may not have admitted that, but that's how it is.)

The fine print on many of these credit guarantee agreements obligates you for other debts incurred by this person, increases in the credit line, and refinancing.

Loan payments are missed, the loan goes into default, and you may not even know about it until you're served with papers demanding you "Pay up!"

Your credit rating may take a hit, other borrowing you need (for a home or automobile) may be affected, and of course you are liable for that person's debt. Even worse: Your relationship could go sour along with the loan.

*Don't do it.*

Just tell them, "Granddaddy told me I should never cosign a loan for anyone."

## 5.18. Is Bankruptcy Ever an Option?

Bankruptcy is for debt builders. They over-extend and can't figure a way out. So they use bankruptcy to wipe the slate clean. It's a legal way to stiff the creditors who trusted they would be paid.

I speak from experience. I've been stiffed by good friends who owed me money, then declared bankruptcy. I understand their position; I forgave them as well as the debt, and I'm glad they got a fresh start. But it's not a happy feeling.

---

*Bankruptcy cannot be an option.*

---

When you take the Wealth Builder approach, you have two factors going for you that make sure you'll never face bankruptcy:

First, you don't get into debt. You live frugally and avoid debt. You're smart enough to get by on 70% of your net income.

You mortgage your home purchase, but you make sure it's a prudent investment and you pay it off early. You may finance a car but, again, you make a prudent purchase, fitting the payments into your living budget, and you pay it off early. So you have no need for bankruptcy.

Second, bankruptcy would devastate your wealth accumulation and you'd have to start over, losing not only the money but some of the time advantage for growing your investments. You don't want that.

## 5.19. Stay Away From Bitcoin

Don't use Bitcoin, and don't invest in it.

Bitcoin is a way of transmitting money online. It's been set up very effectively but it's really a replacement for a check or a bankcard, but without the bank.

I'm not real high on banks but they are backed by the government and I have a much higher trust level for a bank than for a non-bank when it comes to handling my money.

## 5.20. Be Healthy

Without your health, none of this means a thing.

When I was 21, I thought my health was strong (and it was) and that I would live forever (I won't). Looking back, I know I could have done better with my health.

---

*One of the biggest hits on your health is stress. Stress comes in many forms, and finance is one of the biggest. Managing a business takes a big toll, as does struggling with your personal finances when you're in debt.*

---

I'd have been ahead working for someone else and putting aside my 30% to buy shares of big business. It would have left me the time for more exercise, including the basic active lifestyle that's probably most important for physical and mental health. And I could have eaten better to feed my body nutrients it needed, rather than feeding the sugar cravings that loaded it up with too many carbohydrates (and too much ketchup).

You have only one body and one brain; they both have to last you a lifetime.

If you don't take care of them, if you let the maintenance of your body and mind slide, you'll be a mess in 40 years.

It's what you do right now, today and every day, that determines how you'll be doing in 10 years, 20 years, 30 years, and beyond. What you do later may help, but this is another area where starting early makes all the difference.

# 6. Getting Going

We've discussed wealth, credit, and investing, and now you're ready to get started. Great! This is where I'll go over the actual steps you need to take to get things rolling.

We'll start by looking at your debt situation. If you don't have any debt, you can jump ahead to 6.2, *How Do You Actually Start?*

## 6.1.   Is Your Credit Already Screwed Up?

Some counselors advise that you shouldn't start investing until you're completely out of debt.

I asked one of these guys at lunch the other day if that includes home mortgage debt. His answer, "Well, that's okay as long as the interest rate is pretty low."

I asked about an auto loan. His answer, "No, the car should be paid off."

Since you're itching to start investing you'll be happy to know that I disagree... to a point. The challenge is this: If you're busy paying off debt, especially high-interest debt, it probably eats up more cash than you can make investing.

That's why it's a bad thing to have debt.

But it's a good thing to get started with your investments. Otherwise, you might not get started.

If you have debt that doesn't fit conveniently into the 70% spending plan, you'll want to look at the article in the *Appendix* of this book titled, *Getting Out of Debt*.

Most of us Americans have screwed up our credit at some point, so getting out of debt is not a bad thing. It's just a situation. If you're there now, that's okay. It's just a situation to fix.

## 6.2.  How Do You Actually Start?

Start by contacting a low-fee investment company like Fidelity or Vanguard that features low-expense mutual funds, and making a deposit (by check) to open an account with your first monthly investment. Fidelity and Vanguard are *brokerage houses*, but unlike most brokerages, they don't have stock brokers who try to sell you stocks. They just take orders.

Fidelity and Vanguard do business by phone and online. Fidelity also has a number of offices around the country; you can call for an appointment if you want to do business in person.

I started in 1983 in rural Colorado, and it was before the internet, so I did everything by phone and they mailed out the paperwork. That worked out nicely.

I'll explain more in the checklist, 6.3 *Making the Investment Using Our Plan – Step-by-Step*.

### 6.2.1.  *How and Why to Have Multiple Accounts*

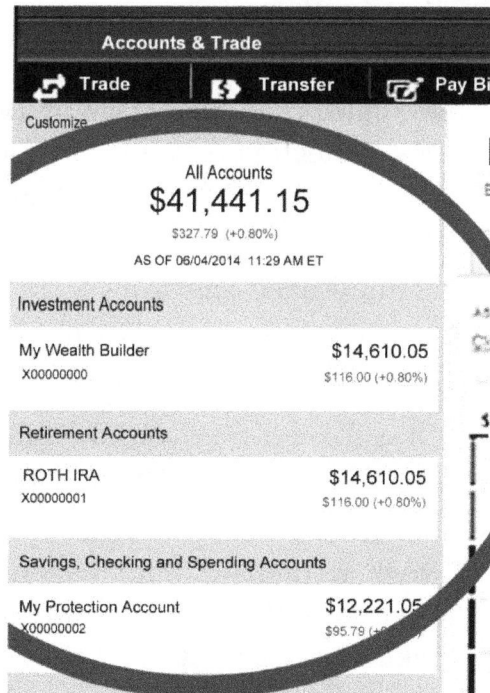

You'll start with one account, but as your investing grows you can open additional brokerage accounts at the same brokerage house. Those can be grouped logically and managed together online. This helps you track your investments for retirement, wealth building, and protection.

Let me clarify: You're the owner. You can have multiple accounts, and in each account you can hold more than one security (mutual fund). The brokerage accounts can be grouped for your convenience.

In this example of a Fidelity investment we suggest three group names already available in the Fidelity website, "Investment Accounts," "Retirement Accounts," and "Savings, Checking and Spending Accounts." Here's an example:

- Investment Accounts (Group)
  - My Wealth Builder (Account)
    - ✓ Spartan 500 Index Fund (Mutual Fund)
- Retirement Accounts (Group)
  - Roth IRA (Account)
    - ✓ Spartan 500 Index Fund (Mutual Fund)
- Savings, Checking, and Spending Accounts (Group)
  - My Protection Account (Account)
    - ✓ Spartan 500 Index Fund (Mutual Fund)

In each group, we've placed the appropriate brokerage or IRA account, and "nicknamed" each so we can readily identify it. "My Protection Account" is much easier to work with than an account named "JT WROS" or "INDIVIDUAL." If you and your spouse each have an IRA account, they'll both be grouped under "Retirement Accounts."

Then, in each account is a mutual fund called *Spartan 500 Index Fund*.

If you follow Strategy B and invest in sector funds in addition to the index fund, those additional fund investments would be listed in each account along with the index funds.

By having multiple accounts you can keep track of how much you have in retirement, in wealth, and in protection. And by having them linked under your login you'll be able to manage them all in one place online.

If you have trouble viewing all your accounts online in a single view, you just call your investment company and ask them to set it up. If you're married, each of you will have to sign paperwork authorizing viewing and making transactions on the other's behalf.

### 6.2.2.  *Get a Cash Account, Not a Margin Account*

For your brokerage accounts you want a *Cash* account, not a *Margin* account. A Cash account is the normal account, but *if* you get asked about Margin, the answer is "no."

A Margin account means it's a credit account; you can borrow against certain holdings to buy additional investments or to get cash. That defeats the purpose and can leave you in big financial trouble. You *may* get offered a Margin account; stick with a *Cash* account.

### 6.2.3.  *Your Account is 'Self-Directed'*

Your investment company might call you or write you and try to sell you managed services, for which they charge a "small" fee. Even in low cost investment companies like Fidelity and Vanguard, they would like to sell you additional services. While it may be nice to know you have that option if you need it, you shouldn't need it.

Then, as your account grows, they will probably try to sell you services again.

---

*'Self-directed' is the industry term that tells them you know how you want to invest your money, you mean what you say, and you want to be left alone.*

---

Just tell them, "My account is *self-directed*; I'm not interested." Thank them and end the call.

### 6.2.4.  *Do You Need a Stock Broker?*

No.

My dad and I have both have had the same experience: Stocks recommended by stock brokers seldom pay off.

I've bought recommended stocks that *did* go up. I've bought recommended stocks that didn't.

Dad's story makes the point. In 1989 he visited me in Phoenix and saw a Home Depot store. He was impressed with their operation, so when he returned home he did some research into their stock and decided to invest.

He called his stock broker, and the stock broker talked him out of it, suggesting another stock instead. Dad followed the broker's advice. The broker's suggested stock tanked, and Home Depot grew. Substantially.

Dad says he really regrets being swayed by the broker. He quit doing business with the broker and started using Fidelity as a low-cost brokerage with substantially lower fees and no attempts to sway his decisions.

Yes, regular stock brokers charge a commission when you buy stocks, or they sell mutual funds that have a load and high expenses. In fact, the commissions are how they make money, so they're most interested in having you buy and sell frequently so they earn lots of commissions.

You want to stick with a well-established, low-cost brokerage with their own no-load mutual funds where you manage your own account. That's why I talk about Fidelity and Vanguard.

### 6.2.5. *Beware of Investment Advisors and Hot Tips*

I don't want to suggest that using a *fee-only* financial advisor is a bad idea. Well... *maybe* I do want to suggest that.

The argument is that a good advisor is worth her fee. "Decades of academic research shows that this is just not true," according to Bo Lu, co-founder of *FutureAdvisor*, an online provider of financial advice. Writing for *Forbes* (May 7, 2012), he says, "The simple math is that an advisor must outperform the market by 1% a year, year after year, just for me to break even after her fees are taken out. Given that low-cost index funds managed by computers beat the most well-compensated money managers on Wall Street 9 times out of 10, I have little confidence that my advisor down the street can do any better, much less beat the market by more than her fees."

I would ask, "If that advisor is so good, why is she peddling her services when she could be investing her own money and reaping the rewards?"

That one percent may sound small but it is a steep price, too. Over 40 years it may cost you more than 25% of the nest egg you expect to have at retirement. (It's no wonder banks and other financial service firms make so much money.)

Of course, there really are a few financial advisors who are worth their fee. The good ones are called fiduciaries, which means they're supposed to put your interests ahead of their own. (There are lots of titles and certifications, like "financial planner," "Certified Financial Planner," etc., but in the end they mean little.) Even within the ranks of fiduciaries there are only a few worthy of your trust, so they're hard to find. If you choose the wrong advisor, it could cost you a big chunk of your investments. By the time you can afford one, you should be comfortably certain that you don't need one.

And take care not to fall for the sucker pitch by marketers who call on the phone or mail you "free dinner" seminar invitations.

This advice includes rejecting the *for-fee* financial advisor that might be offered by Fidelity, Vanguard, or another investment company where you may invest. The information you need you can find online or from the investment company representative at no charge.

Don't pay a fee. You can do better on your own.

There's another type of financial advisor you should know about, the *commission-based* advisors who make their money by selling you high-fee mutual funds, annuities, and life insurance. Sometimes these guys will tell you there's "no fee," or that "the insurance companies pay me."

In fact, it seems as if the salesmen hawking these products all like to call themselves "financial advisors" because they think it sounds so much better than "insurance salesman." In my mind, they're not financial advisors; they are salesmen working to make a commission. They can't legally call themselves a "fiduciary."

There are even a few bold hucksters who try to promote themselves as "for-fee" financial advisors and they *also* take a commission on products they sell. We call them *double dippers*.

There's no need to buy a high-fee mutual fund, or to buy insurance products from a salesman who stands to make a big commission. If you need mutual funds, buy directly from a low-cost mutual fund firm like Fidelity or Vanguard. If you need life insurance, shop online and cut out the commissions. If you need a bank CD, check your low-cost broker (Fidelity or Vanguard) and also shop a site like Bankrate.com to find the best rates. You live in magical times where you can shop in a few seconds online.

Be aware that fraudsters lurk online, though, and do your transactions with major firms and banks... but deal direct, not through an agent.

## 6.3.  Making the Investment Using Our Plan – Step-by-Step

Fidelity and Vanguard are both good investment companies with low fees for index funds and other mutual funds. Dad and I use Fidelity but Mom likes Vanguard, so we're a family that has used both! *If you're going to follow Strategy B, you'll probably want to use Fidelity; Vanguard has very few sector fund choices.*

Choose one – Fidelity or Vanguard – for your investment company.

**Fidelity:** Website: *fidelity.com*   Phone: *800-343-3548*

**Vanguard:** Website: *vanguard.com*   Phone: *800-319-4254*

### 6.3.1.  Strategy A

The easiest investment plan involves using a low cost S&P 500 Index tracking fund. Fidelity's fund is called *Fidelity Spartan 500 Index Fund - Investor Class*. Vanguard's fund is called *Vanguard 500 Index Fund Investor Shares*.

Managing this is pretty easy. You'll start with one account, and expand as your investment grows to the three accounts (Retirement, Wealth, and Protection).

#### Putting Cash in Your Investment Accounts

For all the talk about putting cash in your account, you should know you can't actually deposit *cash*. Instead, use your personal check to open the account.

For additional deposits, you can mail checks or set up an *electronic funds transfer*, or *EFT*, so your investment company can transfer funds to and from your local bank account. That's faster and more secure.

**1. Open an account with your initial investment**. If you're married, this should probably be a joint account, which means you and your spouse jointly own it.

You need enough money to buy a mutual fund ($2,500 at Fidelity; $3,000 at Vanguard). That's probably more than you're ready to invest as you begin. Here's how to go about it:

### At Fidelity

*a. Call Fidelity or go online* and open a *Cash Management Account* with whatever amount you have as your first monthly investment, even if it's less than $2,500. You can open an account with no minimum and your deposit will be held as cash until you have enough to invest in a mutual fund. Then, when you buy your first mutual fund, the fund also will be held in this account.

By the way, they make a big deal of free checking, debit cards, and bill pay services. You don't need most of that at this point, maybe not until you retire. You can use free checking and link your Fidelity account to your bank account so you can easily transfer money back and forth.

*b. Add to this account each payday* or each month until your balance exceeds $2,500 (the minimum to buy into the mutual fund).

*c. Invest in your index fund*. In a few months when you have over $2,500 to invest, call Fidelity or go online and use the cash in the account to buy *Fidelity Spartan 500 Index Fund – Investor Class* mutual fund.

### At Vanguard

*a. Call Vanguard or go online* and open a *Vanguard Brokerage Account* with whatever amount you have as your first monthly investment, even if it's less than $3,000. You can open an account with no minimum and your deposit will be held in a money market settlement fund until you have enough to invest in a mutual fund. Then when you buy your first mutual fund, the fund also will be held in this account.

You can obtain free check writing services and link your Vanguard account to your bank account so you can easily transfer money back and forth.

*b. Add to this account each payday* or each month until your balance exceeds $3,000 (The minimum to buy the Vanguard 500 Index Fund).

*c. Invest in your index fund*. In a few months when you have over $3,000 to invest, call Vanguard or go online and use the money in your settlement fund to buy the *Vanguard 500 Index Fund - Investor Share Class*.

You really want this account to put money in... not to take it out!

When you open your account, be sure your online username and password are as long as they let you make them, have letters *and* numbers, don't match up to any other online logins, and can't be guessed. Your personal wealth is protected by that login; don't be lazy about passwords.

**2. Continue your monthly investments.** Once you own the fund, you can add investments in amounts smaller than the minimum. Continue your monthly investments, adding the funds directly to your index fund. The total values will now go up and down with market fluctuations.

**3. When your investment is big enough, split it into several accounts**. After a few more months the value should reach nine or ten thousand dollars. It's time to split the funds into your Retirement, Wealth, and Protection accounts.

### Your Retirement Account

If your tax advisor says you can, use a Roth IRA as your Retirement account and add funds each year up to the limit by transferring cash into the IRA, then use the cash in the IRA to invest in the Index Fund. Your IRA should be grouped with your "Retirement" brokerage account to simplify management. You are limited to adding $5,500 to your IRA each year. (This limit will probably change every so often.)

Unlike your other accounts, IRAs are not joint accounts so you'll open this for yourself as individual ownership. Your spouse may also qualify, even if your spouse doesn't have a job. If so, open an account for your spouse after a few months when you have the cash. You can add funds up to another $5,500 each year, doubling how much you can invest in a tax-advantaged account. Again, check with your tax advisor about this.

The IRA has significant tax advantages, but you cannot take money out until you're nearing retirement, so be aware of this restriction. Since this investment is intended to be kept until you reach retirement age, this should not be a problem.

If the rules indicate you can't use an IRA, open a Brokerage Account to use as your retirement account.

### Your Wealth Account

For your wealth account you want to open a Brokerage Account.

### Your Protection Account

Your initial account will be used as your Protection Account, so you'll *leave* one-third in the account to start building toward your minimum protection balance.

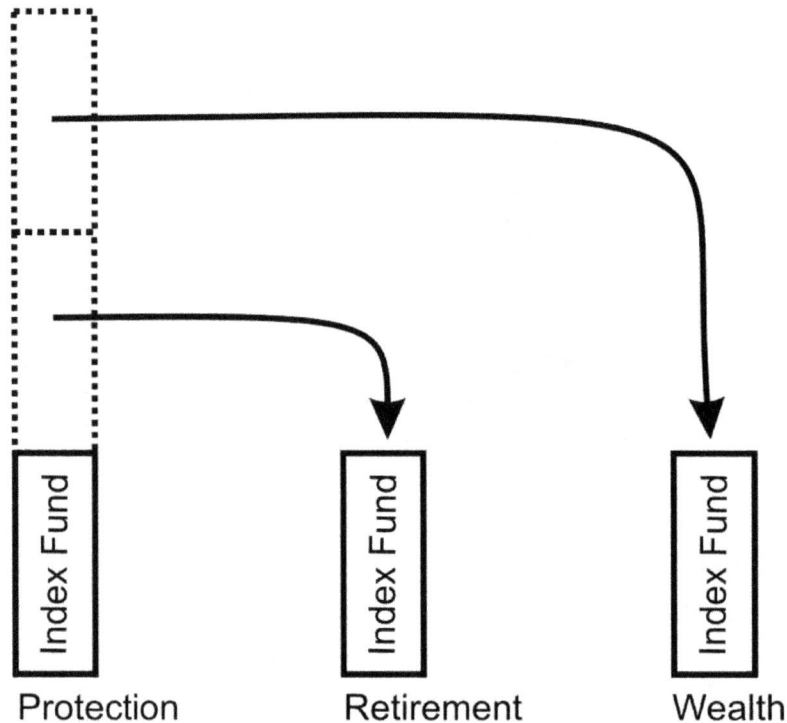

Protection          Retirement          Wealth

**Call your investment company** and tell them about the additional accounts you want to open. You want them grouped under your ownership so they can be easily managed.

Move one-third of your holdings into the IRAs or into the Brokerage Account you set up for retirement, and another one-third into the Brokerage Account you set up for your wealth account.

IRAs require a cash deposit, so you'll have to sell enough of your mutual fund to fund the IRAs, then invest that money inside the IRA account in the Spartan 500 Index Fund.

To transfer into the new Brokerage Accounts tell the representative to move the shares of the index fund "in kind" to the new accounts so there are no tax consequences.

**4. Continue making the monthly investment**. Place one-third of the amount in your retirement accounts, one-third in your Wealth account, and one-third in your Protection account, and invest the funds inside each account in the index fund.

**5. As each index fund balance exceeds $10,000**, call your investment company and ask them to convert the *Investor* shares to *Advantage Class* (Fidelity) or *Admiral shares* (Vanguard) which will reduce your fund expenses nearly in half.

Larger investments are less expensive to manage and they pass these savings on to you. There should be no tax consequences. You'll never get a bill for the expenses; they are deducted from your balance automatically.

Continue to make your monthly investments by having them added to the new fund.

### 6.3.2. *Strategy B*

Strategy B is like Strategy A only you spread some of your investment to sector funds.

**1. Start by following the instructions for Strategy A**. Get your accounts opened and your index fund investments started. Follow steps *one through four* in the Strategy A list.

**2. Decide which sector funds you think are right for you**. In Strategy B, you choose up to three sector funds and put 20% of each investment into each chosen fund. Then you invest the rest, 40% if you've chosen three sector funds, in the index fund. This keeps you strategically diversified. (You don't have to choose three sectors. It's okay to choose just one or two sector funds. Still invest only 20% in each and put the rest in the index fund.)

Review the chapter titled *How to Choose an Actively Managed Mutual Fund*.

**3. As each index fund investment reaches about $9,000**, call your investment company and tell them to sell $3,000 of your index fund and use that to buy your first sector fund.

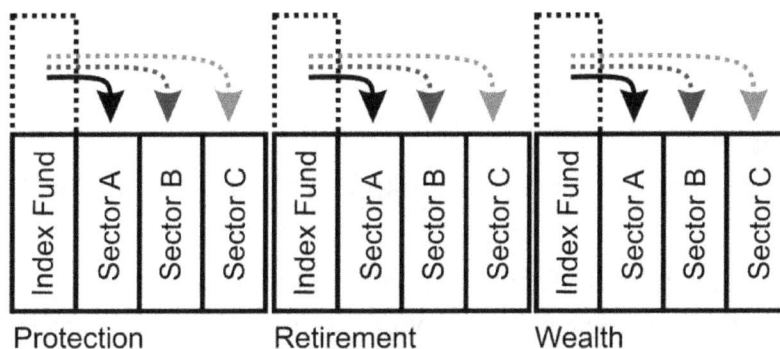

Repeat this step (when you have again reached $9,000) until you've started investing in all three sector funds in each account (protection, retirement, and wealth).

**4. Continue making your monthly investment**. In each group (retirement, wealth, and protection) put 20% in each sector fund and the rest in the Index Fund.

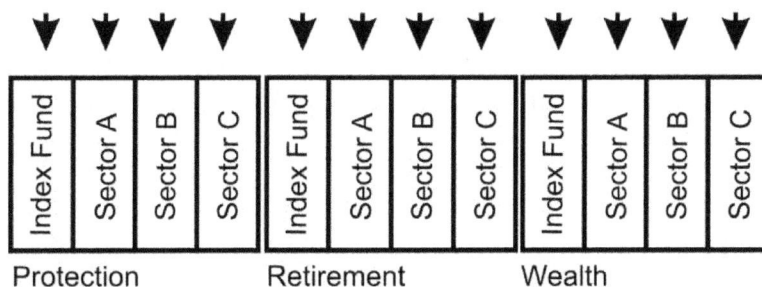

It may seem hard to invest in 12 funds each month, but you make one deposit each month, then call Fidelity or Vanguard or go online to allocate that investment among the funds in your various accounts.

It's also possible to set up automatic investing so the money is transferred from your bank monthly and invested in your designated funds.

**5. As each index fund balance exceeds $10,000**, call your investment company and ask them to convert the *Investor* shares to *Advantage Class* (Fidelity) or *Admiral shares* (Vanguard) which will reduce your fund expenses nearly in half.

Continue to make your monthly investments by having them added to the new fund.

## 6.4. Retiring Right

It wouldn't be fair to go into a wealth building plan without a view toward the end game, your retirement.

---

*Retiring right means retiring in comfort and holding onto your wealth.*

---

You want your wealth to last until *after* you die! Yes, that means having money left over which you can leave to family or charity.

Sometimes I hear people say, "You can't take it with you so why do I want to continue to hold on to the money?"

While it's true you can't take it with you, there's another side to the equation. You certainly don't want it to run out several years before you die, right? Well, since you can't calculate the date you'll die, it's a better choice to plan it so you have some left.

As a Wealth Builder, it would be good to have *a lot* left. You're building wealth, remember?

### 6.4.1. *How Much of Your Wealth Should You Spend in Retirement?*

After all, you did build up your retirement fund so you could retire, right? Retired, we'll hope you also have a Wealth Account and a sizeable Protection Account.

Earlier, I wrote that at retirement if you had enough invested you could live on the earnings. I used a four percent figure. What I'm about to share with you uses different math, but four percent is still the figure.

> *For financial planners, the gold standard is 4 percent. You can afford to spend 4 percent of your savings in the first year you retire. In each subsequent year, you'd withdraw the same amount that you took the previous year, plus an increase for inflation. If you stick to that rule and are properly invested, your money should last for at least 30 years and, in most cases, much longer. You should be financially safe.*
>
> *– Jane Bryant Quinn, AARP Bulletin, Sept., 2014*

While four percent may be the standard, various advisors' suggestions range from 2.5 percent to 5.5 percent. The difference is based on how you keep your money invested and how able you are to adjust to a lower withdrawal if markets decline.

What does it mean to be "properly invested?" Warren Buffet's instruction on the inheritance he leaves his heirs was 10% in bonds, 90% in an S&P 500 tracking stock fund.

Earlier I also gave you an example of retiring with 2.5 million in today's dollars. Since we are going through this now so you can have an understanding of the end game, these retirement illustrations are still in today's dollars.

That 2.5 million dollars in investments would mean you would draw $100,000 the first year, then continue drawing that amount each year, adjusting for inflation.

All these calculations are before taxes.

### 6.4.2.  Running the Business of Your Life in Retirement

At retirement we hope you have three things going for you in addition to your investments:

- Social Security. No one knows how much more damage politicians will do to Social Security but as long as the politicians are afraid to take it away, you should have a decent monthly benefit.

- A pension or 401-K. A pension plan through your employment should provide another monthly benefit. A 401-K can be rolled into an IRA so you can manage it yourself, and you can set up a monthly withdrawal to help with expenses.

- Your home mortgage, cars, and student loans should be long paid off and you should have zero debt.

Those three things should give you a livable cash flow. Remain frugal.

The rest is for comfort and fun, including money to travel several times a year.

I have a good friend who invested well and lives in a modest home, drives an intermediate sedan, and leads a nice, comfortable life. Two or three times a year he takes a month-long vacation with his friends. At other times he takes shorter trips to visit family and friends, or to relax at a resort location. (I think he likes Hawaii best.)

His neighbors know him as a friendly, retired guy who travels some. He's a decamillionaire but there's no hint of wealth. In fact, he has and does everything he wants.

### 6.4.3.  What If You Don't Need the Whole 4 Percent?

Don't use it all. Keep it invested. Let it grow. You might need it later for long-term care or some emergency.

### 6.4.4. *When Should You Start to Draw Social Security?*

A good friend of our family started taking her Social Security when she turned 62 because, she said at the time, "They will let me, and I really need the money." If she had waited, she would get almost twice the money for the rest of her life. I know her well enough to know she "needs the money" more now, but she's stuck with the smaller payments.

Social Security has a "full retirement age" where you normally start getting benefits. For me, it's 66. (For you it will be 67 or older.)

As I write this I could have started drawing Social Security as early as 62. Taking that option would cost me, though, as benefits would be reduced by about 25 percent. That means I would lose about a fourth of what I would receive by starting early.

I can wait until I am 70 to start, and by doing so the benefit grows by eight percent each year. That's four extra years at eight percent a year, 32% more. So I'll get about a third more by waiting.

Here's an example; we'll pretend my "full" age 66 benefit would be $1,500.

If I start at 62, I'd get $1,125. If I wait to 70, I'd get $1,980.

Waiting, as opposed to starting early, is worth $855 a month for the rest of my life. That's 76% more than the amount I would get if I started at 62.

Can I wait? You bet!

These rules will change so read up before you start drawing Social Security. And the numbers vary depending on your earnings history and year of birth. The important thing to remember is to check it out as you approach retirement and make an intelligent choice.

These calculations are made using Social Security's publication, *Effect of Early or Delayed Retirement on Retirement Benefit*, published in 2010.

If you're married, under certain circumstances one spouse may be able to draw Social Security as spousal benefits while waiting to reach age 70 when the higher benefit would kick in. You'll have to check with the Social Security office about that at that time. (I find AARP is a good resource, also.)

### 6.4.5. *What About Minimum Required Withdrawals?*

The IRS has rules for 401-K Plans and traditional IRAs that require you to withdraw a certain amount once you reach the age 70 years six months. (These rules will probably change somewhat by the time you retire.)

The investment company that manages your retirement accounts will tell you about the minimum you must withdraw each year. Be sure to do that. If you miss a deadline, there's a penalty that takes most of the money you should have withdrawn.

The easy way is to have them automatically do the withdrawal before year-end. Dad has his done each November; that way it has most of the year to grow but still gets handled well before year-end. If it's sizeable, you might want it done monthly. The management firm can reinvest it outside your retirement account or deposit it in your checking account.

### 6.4.6. *What About Financial Independence and Retiring Early?*

We talked earlier about how you could retire early if you are financially independent and have enough investments to pay all your expenses for the rest of your life. You can do that but there are a few things to consider:

You have to have accumulated a lot of wealth, enough to safely fund the rest of your life.

You won't be able to tap IRAs or other tax-enhanced retirement accounts until you reach a prescribed retirement age. Nor will you have Social Security or pension money. That's fine; it just means you need to fully fund your early retirement from your wealth account.

You need to have enough invested so that after you make a withdrawal you still have enough to grow and provide a growing fund for the rest of your life.

That means the four percent we've been talking about won't hack it. You need to conserve and protect your investments and keep them growing. You may need to live on one or two percent of your investments to make that happen.

You also need to maintain extra flexibility. That means if there is a downturn in the market or you incur expenses beyond what you expect, you may need to take a part time job to carry you over to better times.

This should not discourage you. Rather, I hope you are encouraged to invest successfully and enable a comfortable and robust retirement.

# 7.  What's Most Important

## 7.1.    Be Happy

What I want for you most of all is that you are happy.

It's a choice. Your choice.

## 7.2.    When to Start

Start now.

It's never too late.

Time and compound interest are the keys to building wealth, but it's never too late to start.

I started at 35.

If you're 20, start now and enjoy immense wealth when you reach retirement, profiting by the magic of 40, 50, or more years of compound growth.

If you're 45, it's not too late to start; the end benefits will just be smaller. You still have the opportunity to be a *Power Wealth Builder*. At this age your children are out of the house, the house should be nearly paid off, and anything you're paying for your children's college should be about done.

Divert that money to your investment program in addition to the 30% Wealth Builder investments and you can catch up pretty fast. No, you won't have the advantage of the previous 25 years of compound growth, but you can still build considerable wealth.

If you're 55 or 60 and nearing retirement, it's *still* not too late.

In fact, with so many people living to be in their 90s and 100s, at 60 or 70 you may still have 30 or 40 years left. Your strategy might be a little different. Finding 500 or 1,000 dollars to invest each month is harder if you're living on Social Security. But you might be able to take on a light job to earn that much, and use it to build wealth.

The idea that you should be enjoying the money now that you've retired makes it hard to invest. Get over that and be a Wealth Builder.

## 7.3.    It's a Decision... 'Live Long and Prosper!'

Spock's *Star Trek* blessing, "Live long and prosper!" is a powerful message. In some translations of the *Bible*, Deuteronomy 5:33 includes "live and prosper" as part of Moses' instructions to the Hebrew people. William Shakespeare's *Romeo and Juliet* contains Romeo's bidding to Balthasar, "Live and be prosperous: and farewell good fellow."

---

*The point is that prosperity is a good thing, worthy of your pursuit.*

---

Do you have to follow the plan perfectly? I certainly didn't. Of course, I didn't have this plan.

There are lots of folks out there with other ideas about how to build wealth, many from prominent advisors, some from publications like *Money* and *USA Today*, and some in books you'll find at the bookstore. Some of these ideas may even work. Some I've tried. A few even made some profit.

For example, you might read about Coca-Cola and decide you would be wise to invest in Coca-Cola, so you buy some shares of Coca-Cola. That's fine, but now you have a specific investment that you need to track. What happens if carbonated drinks lose their attraction, some other companies pick up the beverage market, and the Coca-Cola stock drops? You lose. When should you sell that stock? What should you buy to replace it? More decisions, more work.

But if you've invested in an S&P 500 tracking fund you've invested *indirectly* in Coca-Cola because it's part of the index, and if it loses status as one of the top 500 companies the fund managers will sell and replace it with the new company that replaces it. You don't have to do a thing; you don't even have to make a decision. *You don't even have to know about it!*

Just keep investing.

What I've shared here is *the easy way*.

Down the road, if you decide to invest some of your money in a particular stock or other investment rather than investing in companies through mutual funds, it's okay. It won't ruin you, especially if you keep most of your investments in solid funds.

A little side investment might be really good. I mentioned my cousin, Kathy, who lived in Omaha down the street from Warren Buffett. If she had bought just 10 shares of stock in his company at $260 each in 1980, the investment would be worth over two million dollars today. Of course, Buffett's company is a stellar story, not a typical example.

I hope you'll avoid gambling in the stock market, buying a company to sell in a few days or weeks or months at a profit. The folks that do that are considered *traders*. It's better to be an *investor* who buys a company to keep, or, who buys a fund to keep. Always think long term.

And remember what I've shared. If I had this life to do over with what I know now, the plan in this letter is *exactly* what I'd do.

None of us get to use our own 20-20 hindsight, but you have an opportunity to use mine.

We've covered several things.

1. The mindset of being wealthy and how to become a Wealth Builder.

2. The plan for financial success and an understanding of credit, getting a job and investing a portion of your income and letting it grow to build wealth.

3. How owning big companies is the best way to create wealth, and two easy-to-use strategies for successful investing.

4. Living life as a Wealth Builder, including a look ahead at retirement.

5. Step-by-step instructions on how to get started.

Becoming a Wealth Builder involves investing and there's always some risk in that. I firmly believe these strategies will minimize your risk. You have the plan. Like a diet that occasionally gets ignored, you can still prosper if you follow the plan *most* of the time. The plan is really solid.

It's up to you. It's your decision, one you must make and stubbornly defend.

I wish for you great success and prosperity.


*With Love,*


*Granddaddy*

---------------------------------------

Dear Reader,

I hope you enjoyed *Secret Wealth*. I have to tell you, I really love the simplicity of Strategy A, the strength of the 10-10-10 plan, and the idea that there's such a big difference between building wealth and building debt.

When I wrote *Secret Wealth*, I got so many fans thanking me for the book.

As an author, I love feedback. So tell me what you loved, what you hated. I'd love to hear from you. You can write me at SecretWealth.com/contact and visit me on the web at SecretWealth.com.

Finally, I need to ask a favor. If you're so inclined, I'd love a review of *Secret Wealth*. Loved it, hated it – I'd just enjoy your feedback.

As you may have gleaned from my books, reviews can be tough to come by these days. You, the reader, have the power now to make or break a book. If you have the time, here's a link to my Author Page on Amazon: amazon.com/author/richhamilton

Thank you so much for reading Secret Wealth and for spending time with me.


In gratitude,


Rich Hamilton
*P.S.: Appendix follows.*

---------------------------------------

# Appendix

## Appendix A.  Key Concepts

**Be a Wealth Builder, Not a Debt Builder**. Debt is your enemy. Reverse it and build wealth instead.

**Time is Your Biggest Asset; Use it Wisely**. The magic secret which I revealed precisely in these pages is that by taking action now and using time profitably you can have time do most of the work for you as you build wealth.

**Pay Yourself First; Use the 10-10-10 Investment Plan**. Get a good job. As you earn money invest first for your retirement, wealth, and protection; spend the rest on your lifestyle.

**Live Frugally**. Spend within your means. Create a Spending Plan that provides for a reasonable lifestyle after investing for your future.

**Build Wealth and Let the Money it Generates Fund Your Spending**. Accumulating money is not your ultimate goal. Ultimately you want to spend money. Done right, you will accumulate money and let that accumulated money work for you; eventually you'll spend a portion of the money it generates on the things that fit with your values and desires. That's what building wealth is about.

**Being a Great Investor is Hard**. But being a smart investor is easy. Use low-expense index-based mutual funds and carefully selected sector mutual funds to grow your wealth.

**Keep Your Financial Business a Secret**. Never tell your children their parents are wealthy. Teach them discipline and frugality. Teach them about saving, investing, and liquidity.

Don't try to compete with your children, your relatives, or your friends. Never boast about how much you have accumulated. Buy things conservatively. Avoid flash;keep a low profile.

A common thought should be:

*"People would be astonished at how much wealth I have accumulated. I know how to hang on to it."*

## Appendix B.  Is the 10-10-10 Plan Too Aggressive?

You might be concerned that my 10-10-10 Investment Plan is too aggressive in that it adds up to investing 30% of your net check each payday.

Let's explore that.

Most financial advisors suggest saving 15% of your net check for retirement. I'm actually suggesting 10% for retirement plus 10% for wealth building. Combined, that's 20%, not so much more aggressive as you might first think. Since it's intended to make you wealthy, not just provide "enough" for your retirement, I think that's okay and I hope you do, too.

The third 10% is something else entirely. It's for your *Protection Account*. It's designed to hold three years' expenses and additional money for unexpected car repairs, home repairs, medical bills, etc.

You should never dip into your wealth or retirement accounts for unexpected expenses.

I hope you're never unemployed for three years, but if you are, you're covered for that, maybe even longer if you take a temporary job with lower pay while you're job hunting.

You will certainly have unexpected expenses. Maybe you'll be able to cover those out of your 70%, but if you can't, you have a place to get some help without dipping into your primary investments.

Ideally, once the three year minimum is in place, you'll be able to dip into the Protection Account when you need it, funding it again with future paychecks. I'd expect this account to grow and shrink as your needs require.

You'll also have the power of compounded growth helping you keep the Protection Account growing. Yes, if you can, just let it grow and never tap it for any emergencies; then you can celebrate someday with those extra funds.

Whether you're setting aside 15% or 30%, it will seem like a lot and seem impossible but it can be done. Yes, really. I've been there and I thought it impossible, too, so I didn't always do it. But, looking back, I know it could have been different.

Remember what I shared earlier, no matter what you make there are lots of people getting by on 70% of what you're making. If they can do it, you can too. It takes a firm decision.

## Appendix C.  Mutual Funds or Stocks?

I occasionally hear from people who really think you should invest in stocks, not mutual funds, or they question my mutual fund strategy. You'll recall that I said all mutual funds are not created equal. It's also true that all stocks are not created equal, and the big challenge, if you're going to invest in stocks, is picking the right ones.

That's where Warren Buffett excels, choosing the companies he invests in, and he and his staff invest a lot of time and money researching companies and making those choices. As I noted, Buffett is a great investor.

I'm *not* a great investor. In stocks, I've picked some winners, and I've also picked losers.

Mutual funds solve that problem by spreading the risk. A mutual fund invests in hundreds or thousands of companies, and hires managers to do the work. Most funds are *actively managed,* trying to beat the market. A very few succeed at that because that's very hard to do consistently.

The first index fund opened in 1975; John Bogle founded the Vanguard 500 Index Fund to follow an established market index, the S&P 500, made up of 500 leading U.S. companies. An investment in this kind of index fund represents an investment in all 500 companies.

Bogle reasoned that if everyone was trying to beat the S&P 500 and few were succeeding consistently, why not start a fund that duplicates the S&P 500? It works beautifully.

Bogle has said a couple of things which I think are appropriate here.

> *"There are only two guarantees in the financial business. If you buy an index fund you'll get the market return, and if you don't invest at all you'll get nothing."*

Choosing specific companies to invest in holds no guarantee. Likewise, a mutual fund that is not based on an index has no assurance of performance *and* has higher management costs. But buying an index fund will deliver the market return.

In an interview with *The Motley Fool's* Tom Gardner, Bogle talked about how to invest:

> *"You should have a serious money account where you put money in a market index fund and maybe balance it out a bit with some bonds and don't look at it. Don't look at it for 50 years. Don't peek. When you retire, open the envelope. Be sure a doctor is nearby to revive you. You'll go into a dead faint. You won't believe there's that much money in the world."*

I love how Bogle describes an investment that takes virtually no effort on the part of the investor, other than investing funds regularly. That's the idea behind our plan:

- Consistent investing every month or every payday.

- No daily, monthly, or yearly management decisions to make.

- Invested in an index fund that has low expenses and invests in 500 leading U.S. companies.

Bogle points out that if you are 20 now, you will probably live to be 90 or older. That means your investments can continue to grow for 70 or more years. That kind of growth will be mind boggling!

Our Strategy A is simple; invest in the S&P 500 Index fund.

What could be better?

Our Strategy B adds sector funds to that, which means you invest a portion of your money in certain industries and the rest in the S&P 500 Index fund which follows the wide market (all industries).

If... *and that's an important "if"*... you can pick three sectors that will grow faster than the general market, you can bump up your earnings.

There *is* risk in that. Strategy B balances the risk by limiting investment in each sector to 20% and maintaining 40% invested in the index fund.

If one sector goes way down, it's likely that the other sectors will fare better. Another way to look at that is that it's unlikely all three sectors will go down at the same time unless there's a general downturn in all stocks. Even then, if you've picked well, one of your sectors will likely beat the market.

By investing in mutual funds, either using the index fund or a combination of index fund and three sector funds, you're investing in hundreds of companies. And you're taking it easy in that you don't have to give your investments much attention.

*"You don't need to be a rocket scientist. Investing is not a game where the guy with the 160 IQ beats the guy with 130 IQ." – Warren Buffett*

## Appendix D.  Is 13% a Realistic Return?

One of the top financial planners in the country looked at this book and questioned whether I've set expectations too high by suggesting you can get a 13% return on your investments; that's the number I've used in most of my calculations and I think it's a good goal.

But is it realistic? No one knows, because no one can accurately predict the future except to say there will be ups and downs, good times and bad. I know advisors who use 10%, 9%, and 7%. I tend to be a more aggressive investor (that's why there's a Strategy B), so I use 13%.

But let's look at history (mid 2005 to mid 2015).

### A 10 year Flashback

Looking back 10 years includes the 2008 recession, so it should be a very pessimistic look at returns.

If you're using Strategy A and investing only in the index fund, the 10 year return is 8.09%, well below 13%.

If you're using Strategy B it will depend on which sector funds you choose to add to the mix, but here's an example:

- Fidelity Select Healthcare 10 yrs: 15.33%

- Fidelity Select Software and Computer Services 10 yrs: 15.06%

- Fidelity Select Multimedia 10 yrs: 12.06%

- Fidelity Spartan 500 Index Fund 10 yrs: 8.09%

- Strategy B Weighted average: 11.72%

Each of these sectors did better than the overall market, but figuring an average (and allowing for the fact that more is invested in the index fund than in any single sector), the return would be 11.72%. That's still not 13%, but it's a lot closer.

### A 5 year Flashback

Looking back 5 years does not include the 2008 recession, so it should be a very optimistic look at returns.

If you're using Strategy A and investing only in the index fund, the 5 year return is 16.49%, well above 13%.

If you're using Strategy B it will depend on which sector funds you choose, but using the same funds from the previous example:

Fidelity Select Healthcare 5 yrs: 26.63%

Fidelity Select Software and Computer Services 5 yrs: 18.48%

Fidelity Select Multimedia 5 yrs: 19.55%

Fidelity Spartan 500 Index Fund 5 yrs: 16.49%

Strategy B Weighted average: 19.52%

Each of these sectors did better than the overall market, but figuring an average (and allowing for the fact that more is invested in the index fund than in any single sector), the return would be 19.52%. That's a lot more than 13%.

## What's Realistic?

If you follow Strategy A, over the last 25 years the annualized return on the S&P 500 is 9.62%, so getting nearly 10% over the long term is just matching the S&P 500 and that's good!

If you follow Strategy B and pick the right sectors, the intent is that those sectors should outperform the index fund and increase your effective return over the S&P 500 return.

But what's realistic? No one knows; the next 10 - 50 years could be better or could be worse.

I'm sure there will be market corrections but I hope not as dramatic as in 2008. However, over 50 years? A lot can and will happen. But I have faith in American business so I "forecast" somewhere in between.

My forecast carries no authority, however. You could research what "the experts" say but the truth is they don't know either.

Remember how we talked about $1,000 today growing to over $176,000 in 40 years? That's at 13% compound growth. At 10%, that $1,000 would grow to $53,700 in 40 years. I think this shows (a) why you might rather try for 13% *and* (b) how earning 10% is pretty darn good, too.

A friend in our area retired early 30 years ago, invested his retirement money in a healthcare sector mutual fund, and let it grow. Over 30 years, including five market corrections where the market dropped 20% or more, his annual compound growth works out to 16.85%. Putting everything into one sector is risky, but he picked a good sector for that period and it worked.

So... will *you* be able to average 13% or better over the next 40 or 50 years? I don't know and no one else knows, but I know that if you do nothing you'll get nothing. It's better to try.

My wish for you is great success!

*The sector funds listed here are for illustrative purposes only and not listed as a recommendation. You must do your own research to determine which sector funds you want to buy.*

## Appendix E.   Getting Out of Debt

So, you've got a bunch of debt and want to clean it up so you can start a wealth building program?

Great idea!

Most of us have screwed up our credit at some point, including me. It may help you to know that getting out of debt is not a bad thing. It's just a situation, and one you need to fix.

If you're reading this chapter I'm going to assume your debt picture is bad enough that you really don't know what you can do about it. Let's lay out a debt fixing plan that will merge nicely with your investment program when it starts to make sense to invest.

In *The Richest Man in Babylon*, George S. Clason lays out a good plan for paying off debt, including the concept of keeping your spending to 70% or less of your income. His plan is to pay yourself first by investing 10% for retirement, then use 20% to repay debt and the remaining 70% for living expenses, including rent and transportation.

### Take 10% to Start Your Retirement Investment Program

Pay yourself first. A portion of what you make is yours to keep and invest. Start this part of your investment program so you have a handle on your future and won't feel like you're a slave to your debt. You'll only be doing the first leg of the 10-10-10 plan, but it's a beginning!

In addition, start your employer-sponsored 401-K or pension program if it's available where you work. If your employer matches your contribution, do that – *maximize that* – even though you have high interest debt. The employer match is found money, and it's invested along with the amount you put in through payroll deductions. It's not part of the 10-10-10 investment plan and, since it's a payroll deduction, you won't see the money except to know it's invested.

### Take 20% of Your Check to Pay Down Your Debt

Pay off the high interest debt first.

Credit card debt is high interest debt and should be paid off along with other credit accounts before expanding your investment program. Your home mortgage and car payment should be included in your 70% spending plan, not part of this 20% pay-down.

Pay the minimum amount on every account except the one with the highest interest rate, and pay everything you possibly can on that one. This will pay your total debt down faster.

When this debt is paid off you can immediately switch it into your wealth and protection account investments, and your full investment program will be underway.

## Take the Remaining 70% to Spend on Rent, Auto, and Expenses

Start your 70% spending plan by adjusting your spending to 70% (or less) of your net check. If you can make it less than 70%, you can apply more to reduce debt.

**Your home mortgage**. Your house payment is part of your "rent-factor." If you weren't buying a home, you'd be paying rent. The house payment should be factored into your spending plan as part of the 70% of take-home pay, just like other living expenses. Ideally, the house payment will not exceed 25% of take-home pay, and, we hope, you're paying extra each month to get it all paid off early!

**Your car payment**. Your car payment is a transportation expense, one you'll have the rest of your life. It, too, should be at a low rate and be part of your 70% spending plan.

**Discretionary expenses**. This is a time to cut discretionary expenses, even if they fit in the 70%. It's not a time to be paying big cable bills, going on expensive vacations, getting recreational equipment, going out to eat, getting a new pet, or buying new clothes.

These are the kind of things that get us into trouble in the first place. Give these things up and apply the money to paying down the bills faster. Later, after you're debt-free, if you can fit it into your 70% you can resume some of these.

## Emergency Funds

**You should have some emergency funds set aside before you invest**. Dave Ramsey suggests $1,000 plus three to six months of expenses. Suze Orman thinks you should set aside eight months of expenses.

Remember that your Granddaddy thinks a Protection Account is part of your financial plan, so put this money into a cash management account as soon as you can. When it grows to $4,000 or so, move $3,000 into a Spartan 500 Index Fund, keeping $1,000 liquid for unexpected expenses.

There *will* be unexpected expenses, and, by their nature, you can't know what they will be.

While I think three years of expenses should be your goal, you'll recall that can take about 12 years if you're invested right. Start with three months, plus the $1,000. Then grow it to six months, then nine months. Keep it growing by adding to the fund and investing it. You'll get there.

## Should You Sell Assets?

If you own your home and can't afford the payments, you made a mistake that needs to be corrected.

Before you sell, you need to have a realistic grasp on what your home is worth if you sell it, after real estate commissions and other expenses. And you need to know what the loan pay-off is. If you're "upside-down," meaning you owe more than the home is worth, you need some expert help and that's beyond the focus of this letter.

You also need to know how much you'll pay for rent; after all, you have to live somewhere! You'll always have a "rent factor."

I recently saw a show on TV where one friend admitted to another that she settled in Brooklyn because she couldn't afford Manhattan, and that she stays in Brooklyn because now she can't afford to leave. The show was fiction but the situation is real. Sometimes you have to live where you can afford it rather than where you want to live or where you work.

## All Debt is Not Created Equal; How to Handle The Payments

When some folks get in too deep, they make bad judgments about who to pay first and it makes things worse. Some like to start with the biggest bills, some with the smallest. Some will pay on a particular bill first because it's a bill that makes them mad, or maybe it makes them happy. Others will pay the minimum payment plus an extra amount on every bill. None of these make business sense.

There is a strategy that makes good business sense.

First, recognize that making the minimum payment is not enough. It will take years to pay off a bill and during that time you will pay so much interest it's sickening. Minimum payments are established to make the bank money, not to suggest that it's in your best interest to pay only that amount.

Here's the trick: You want to pay the minimum payment on all bills *except one*. On *that bill* you want to pay the minimum *plus* as much as you can possibly add to the payment.

Make a list of everything you owe. Next to each, write down the amount owed, the interest rate (APR, or annual percentage rate), and the minimum payment.

Now, rewrite this list in the order of interest rate, with the highest interest rates at the top.

The point of this exercise is to *pay off the highest interest bills first*, because that will help you make the fastest progress. So... each month, pick the bill with the highest interest rate. Make minimum payments on all the other bills, then pay the minimum plus as much as you possibly can on that highest-rate bill.

When I was paying myself out of debt I made up a little list as suggested above. Then each month as I paid bills I noted in a column by each bill how much interest I paid that month to each account. After paying bills, I added up the interest.

When you're paying off old bills, you're paying for stuff you bought some time ago. The money you pay gets you nothing today. Even worse, the interest gets you nothing at all, and it's something you really can't afford!

Each month I'd look at my list of bills and add up the total amount of interest I'd paid. I'd compare that to previous months.

It's often disheartening to look at the total amount of bills you owe because the balances come down slowly. Comparing the total interest paid monthly is more encouraging because it comes down faster, primarily because you are paying off the high interest bills first.

**There's no "magic bullet."** When you get in a financial jam, it's easy to think you should jump at some "deal" that will generate a bunch of cash to help you or to think you should take that vacation to "clear your head" so you can deal with the problem.

There's no magic bullet. You just need to decrease expenses and pay off bills intelligently so everyone gets paid. Maybe you need to get a second job, part-time, to increase income. Then re-start your life with responsible financial management.

**What if this is not enough?** If your minimum payments add up to more than you can pay, you've got a deeper problem, beyond the scope of this letter. Lenny Tumbarello wrote a book on the subject called *No Balance Due*, but it's hard to find today. Instead, get the book, *Financial Peace* by Dave Ramsay or *The 9 Steps to Financial Freedom* by Suze Orman for advice. Just get the book, and do what it says. There's no need to buy a bunch of books on the topic, or a set of CDs, or an interactive internet website, or to sign up for counseling services. Twenty bucks is your total budget for this task, and it won't cost that much!

## Don't fall for credit repair schemes

When you're in debt, it's natural to want a quick fix.

There is no such thing.

But there are credit repair con artists who do nothing but charge high upfront fees or hidden costs for their "services." AARP warns us to "Beware of individuals or companies promising to 'fix' your credit virtually overnight."

## Appendix F. Warren Buffett Says

Warren Buffet's perspective is sound and the instructions he gives the trustee in his will are simple and precise. Buffett says:

> In aggregate, American business has done wonderfully over time and will continue to do so (though, most assuredly, in unpredictable fits and starts). In the 20th Century, the Dow Jones Industrials index advanced from 66 to 11,497, paying a rising stream of dividends to boot. The 21st Century will witness further gains, almost certain to be substantial. The goal of the non-professional should not be to pick winners – neither he nor his "helpers" can do that – but should rather be to own a cross-section of businesses that in aggregate are bound to do well. A low-cost S&P 500 index fund will achieve this goal.

> "That's the 'what' of investing for the non-professional. The 'when' is also important. The main danger is that the timid or beginning investor will enter the market at a time of extreme exuberance and then become disillusioned when paper losses occur... The antidote to that kind of mistiming is for an investor to accumulate shares over a long period and never to sell when the news is bad and stocks are well off their highs. Following those rules, the 'know-nothing' investor who both diversifies and keeps his costs minimal is virtually certain to get satisfactory results. Indeed, the unsophisticated investor who is realistic about his shortcomings is likely to obtain better long-term results than the knowledgeable professional who is blind to even a single weakness.

> "My money, I should add, is where my mouth is: What I advise here is essentially identical to certain instructions I've laid out in my will... My advice to the trustee could not be more simple: Put 10% of the cash in short-term government bonds and 90% in a very low-cost S&P 500 index fund. (I suggest Vanguard's.) I believe the trust's long-term results from this policy will be superior to those attained by most investors – whether pension funds, institutions or individuals – who employ high-fee managers."

> "Both individuals and institutions will constantly be urged to be active by those who profit from giving advice or effecting transactions. The resulting frictional costs can be huge and, for investors in aggregate, devoid of benefit. So ignore the chatter, keep your costs minimal, and invest in stocks as you would in a farm."

> – Warren Buffett, Berkshire-Hathaway Shareholder Letter (2013)

## Appendix G.  What Banks Do

While your money is safely "in" the bank *they loan your money to other people* at a profit.

This sounds almost criminal, but let me assure you it's all quite legal, and has been made so over centuries by kings and queens and governments who knew how badly their countries needed money invested to build their economies.

The banking system has been designed to *create money* in a way that you can't begin to do yourself. While your money is on deposit in the bank they can loan out 90% of it to someone else, who promptly deposits it in the bank at which point 90% of *that* amount can be loaned to another person. A simplified example might be helpful:

1. You deposit $100,000 in the bank, and 90% of that can be loaned.

2. The bank loans $90,000 to Mark, who deposits it in the bank. Ninety percent of that can be loaned ($81,000), and the bank now has $190,000 in deposits.

3. The bank loans the $81,000 to Michael, who deposits it in the bank. Ninety percent of that can be loaned ($72,900), and the bank now has $271,000 in deposits.

4. The bank loans the $72,900 to Curtis, who deposits it in the bank. Ninety percent of that can be loaned ($65,610), and the bank now has $336,610 in deposits.

5. The bank loans the $65,610 to Karen, who deposits it in the bank. Ninety percent of that can be loaned ($59,049), and the bank now has $395,659 in deposits.

6. The bank loans the $59,049 to Matt, who deposits it in the bank. Ninety percent of that can be loaned ($53,144), and the bank now has $448,803 in deposits.

Thanks to your initial deposit of $100,000 and only five subsequent loans the bank now has $448,803 in deposits. They have "created money" by loaning out most of the deposited money.

As the process continues, your initial $100,000 deposit will actually create enough money that the bank will have about a million dollars in deposits. They pay you very little (or nothing) for the money. Then they loan the money out at much higher rates, including credit card rates as high as 26% or more.

The difference is what the bank generates as profit.

The bank loves it when you deposit money. And they love it when you borrow, because they can charge you so much in interest. And it's not even their money!

What happens when someone who borrowed money spends it on something? The store where they spent the money promptly deposits it in the bank. Net difference to the bank, zero.

## Appendix H.  U.S. Median Income Data

Income per household in 2013:

All households $51,939

15-24 years $34,311

25-34 years $52,702

35-44 years $64,973

45-54 years $67,141

55-64 years $57,538

65 and over $35,611

Ages reflect age of head of household.

Source: U.S. Census Bureau, Current Population Survey, 2014 Annual Social and Economic Supplement.

## Appendix I.   Personal Balance Sheet

Copy and use this form to calculate your personal net worth. See the chapter titled *Understand Your Personal Balance Sheet and Your Net Worth* for instructions.

### ASSETS

Long-Term Assets

_____ $_____

_____ $_____

_____ $_____

Total Long-Term Assets                                    $_____

Liquid Assets

_____ $_____

_____ $_____

_____ $_____

Total Liquid Assets                             $_____

TOTAL ASSETS (Long-Term Assets + Liquid Assets)      $_____

### LIABILITIES

_____ $_____

_____ $_____

_____ $_____

_____ $_____

TOTAL LIABILITIES                              $_____

**NET WORTH** (Total Assets – Total Liabilities)          $_____

## Appendix J.   Personal Cash Flow – Your Personal Spending Plan

Copy and use this form to prepare your Personal Spending Plan.

**INCOME**

Wages (Net Check after deductions)

_____ $_____

_____ $_____

Total Wages $_____

Other Income (If Any)

_____ $_____

_____ $_____

Total Other Income $_____

TOTAL INFLOW (Wages + Other Income) $_____

**INVESTMENT PLAN** (Pay Yourself First) $_____

**EXPENSES**

_____ $_____

_____ $_____

_____ $_____

_____ $_____

_____ $_____

_____ $_____

_____ $_____

_____ $_____

TOTAL EXPENSES $_____

TOTAL OUTFLOWS (Investment Plan + Expenses) $_____

**SURPLUS** (Total Inflows – Total Outflows) $_____

# About the Author

**Rich Hamilton** brings you over 45 years experience as an entrepreneur and expert in sales, marketing, and advertising. Rich has authored over 500 articles and produced and appeared in over 3000 radio programs. He was president of a broadcast communications company, is a qualified systems analyst, and has consulted with hundreds of companies seeking help to increase sales and profits through advertising, marketing, and selling.

Internet: SecretWealth.com

Mail care of: SellBetter Tools Publishing, Box 50186, Phoenix, AZ 85076